Technology Lost

Hype and Reality in the Digital Age

Ron Schneiderman

PH
PTR

Prentice Hall PTR
Upper Saddle River, NJ 07458
www.phptr.com

ISBN 0-13-042203-7

9 780130 422033

A Cataloging-in-Publication Data record for this book can be obtained from the Library of Congress.

Editorial/Production Supervision: *Faye Gemmellaro*
Publisher: *Bernard Goodwin*
Editorial Assistant: *Michelle Vincenti*
Marketing Manager: *Dan DePasquale*
Manufacturing Manager: *Alexis R. Heydt-Long*
Interior Design*: Gail Cocker-Bogusz*
Cover Design Director: *Jerry Votta*
Cover Design: *Anthony Gemmellaro*

Prentice Hall books are widely used by corporations and government agencies for training, marketing, and resale.

For more information regarding corporate and government bulk discounts, contact:

Corporate and Government Sales: (800) 382-3419 or corpsales@pearsontechgroup.com

Printed in the United States of America

10 9 8 7 6 5 4 3 2 1

ISBN 0-13-042203-7

Pearson Education Limited
Pearson Education Australia Pty., Limited
Pearson Education Singapore, Pte. Ltd.
Pearson Education North Asia Ltd.
Pearson Education Canada, Ltd.
Pearson Educatión de Mexico, S.A. de C.V.
Pearson Education—Japan
Pearson Education Malaysia, Pte. Ltd.

Contents

CHAPTER 3
When Technology "Push" Comes To Shove   *81*

CHAPTER 4
Good Examples, Good News   *117*

Introduction:

Riding the Hype Cycle

This book is about promise. It's also about expectations. It's about how new and emerging technologies and high-tech products and services are heavily promoted, sometimes for years, before making it in the marketplace, and then it may be too early or too late.

It often takes years for technologies to develop and even longer to win mass market acceptance. But the list of those that have not quite caught up with the hype, or "gained traction," as one business editor put it, is growing. "At some point," one high-circulation, high-tech magazine editorialized, "this industry has to deliver on its promises, with real products that do something useful and meaningful."

Hype per se isn't a bad thing, Randall Rothenberg, a contributing editor for *Advertising Age,* wrote in one of his columns. "But, like prescription medicine, you've got to know when to use it, lest you overdose. Unfortunately, expectations are usually high and delivery is often slow."

Technology is hard. It takes time, but so does the bureaucracy that inevitably surrounds and occasionally smothers new developments. Thirty-six years passed between the time AT&T announced the development of the concept for cellular communications and its introduction as a commercial service. Sixteen years lapsed between the first demonstration of the computer mouse and the time it was actually shipped with a PC.

Technologies continue to be developed and hyped as the "next big thing." We are assured that we need these new things. They will enrich our lives, make us more productive.

Indeed, we can't do without them. In 1975, McGraw-Hill brought in a bunch of IBM people to pitch the editors of *Electronics* magazine on their new computer terminals. The idea was to link the editors into a network and make it possible for them to actually set type as they were writing their articles. The IBMers were horrified when some of the magazine's editors said they were perfectly happy with typewriters, particularly when they discovered that some of the editors were still using manual typewriters, not IBM Selectrics. *Electronics* was an obvious starting point; getting all of its editors onboard (most of them had engineering backgrounds), writing their articles on IBM terminals, would lead to everyone else in the building eventually adopting the same technology. McGraw-Hill bought into the technology and became a natural showplace for IBM in the publishing community.

Sensor-laden automobiles rely almost entirely on electronics to operate; at least 40% of the value of today's cars, we're told, is in electronics. Car manufacturers pitch new features and functions with each new model year. What used to be options in automobile are increasingly standard features. They're there, whether you want them or not.

Consultants at the Gartner Group, a market research and technology consultancy, have looked closely at this phenomenon. They call it the hype cycle (see Figure I–1). The way Gartner sees it, when a new technology, like the Internet, gets *pushed* into high gear, the hype curve soars upward until it reaches a peak of "inflated expectations." It then begins to sink rapidly into a "trough of disillusionment" as less successful players drop out. It then begins to climb upward again to a new stable plateau as winners begin to emerge and the new technology is adopted by people who understand it and find it useful.

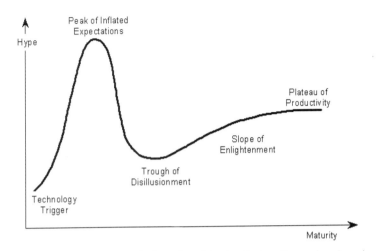

FIGURE I–1 The Hype Cycle, introduced by the Gartner Group, has five phases. The Technology Trigger is a breakthrough, product launch, or other event that generates significant press industry interest. The Peak of Inflated Expectations usually results in unrealistic projections. The Trough of Disillusionment occurs when the technology does not live up to its over-inflated expectations. The Slope of Enlightenment happens when experimentation leads to an understanding of the technology's applicability, and the Plateau of Productivity occurs when the benefits of the technology are demonstrated and accepted. ***Source: Gartner Research.***

Hype isn't among the words in the glossary provided by Emerging*tech*PR.com, a Web site for PR professionals with high-tech clients, but "buzz" made the list. It's defined as "A slang term that describes the excitement surrounding a company or product, often caused by extensive positive media coverage." The Random House dictionary defines hype as "*v.* 1. to stimulate, excite, or agitate. 2. to intensify (publicity) by ingenious or questionable methods. *n.* 3. an ingenious or questionable method used in publicity to intensify the effect." Several magazines that specialize in reporting on technology are so mindful of buzz or hype that they regularly devote editorial space to it. There's *Wired* magazine's "Hype List," which has taken on the task of "deflating this month's overblown memes." The *Industry Standard* used to feature a section called "The Buzz Stops Here" and promoted itself as "99.999% HYPE FREE" in its house ads (which didn't help much; the magazine folded in mid-2001).

UPSIDE features a similar column, called "Buzz Cuts." *Ziff Davis Smart Business* published an appropriately cynical page called the "Hype Detector" with several items per issue, such as, "So how come you don't have interactive TV yet?" Another technology magazine, *Darwin*, simply calls this section "Buzz," but also offers The Darwin Meter so it can actually rate the hype.

You can get closer to the source of much of the hype by checking *PR Watch*, a nonprofit quarterly publication that has been tracking public relations activities since 1993. In June 2001, *PR Watch* launched a free Web site feature called "Spin of the Day." Spin of the Day and *PR Watch* are published by the Center for Media and Democracy, a nonprofit tax-exempt organization based in Madison, Wisconsin. "The purpose of Spin of the Day (www.prwatch.org/cgi/spin.cgi)," says *PR Watch* editor Sheldon Rampton, "is to provide in a timely fashion to both journalists and citizens interested in tracking the often-hidden influence that public relations exerts on the news and public opinion."

Hidden influences? The Association of Competitive Technology (ACT) calls itself a national education and advocacy group for the technology industry, representing mostly small- and medium-sized companies. But according to a *PR Watch* Spin of the Day, it was created and funded by Microsoft to defend itself against U.S. Justice Department charges of antitrust violations. ACT applauded the late June 2001 appeals court ruling reversing the order to break up Microsoft within days of the court's decision. "The court got it right in rejecting the outrageous notion that integration is harmful to consumers and the industry," said ACT President Jonathan Zuck, in a *PR Newswire* release. "Tight integration among related areas of the IT industry promotes competition by enabling low-cost competitors to go toe-to-toe with a high-priced incumbent. Integration has always been an important part of innovation," Zuck said.

Another high-tech PR "think tank" is the Independent Institute and the National Taxpayers Union which, according to *PR Watch*, has received substantial funding from Microsoft while espousing its position regarding the antitrust issue. Some of these financial ties were disclosed when Oracle, one of Microsoft's leading competitors, hired a private investigator to literally dig through ACT's trash in search of incriminating documents.

"Everyone is talking about technology," Marty Cooper, the former Motorola R&D vice president who is largely responsible for the design of the first cellular phone, told *Technology Review*. "What's important is what people do with technology."

It's not always clear why some technologies or products succeed and others do not. It is clear, however, that hype plays an important role in the process. We're not only aware of it; we seem to accept it.

Evidence can be found in three recent headlines—"Overloaded by Wireless Hype?" from *eBusiness Advisor*, "Don't Believe All the Hype" from a *PC Magazine* feature on the wireless Web, and "Hyperencryption: Much Hype About Little That Is New" from *IEEE Spectrum* magazine.

Quotes from technology industry publications support this idea as well. For example, in the *SuperComm2000 Show Daily*, Michael Gallipo, vice president and portfolio manager for Monument Funds Group's Telecommunications Fund, said: "We believe data is the next great future for wireless. The great risk is that the hype outruns the reality." A recent "Our Money Matters" column in the *Wall Street Journal* stated "Overall, we found some of the most hyped features [in 'smart' phones] to be the least useful—or at least several technological leaps away from being useful. That was especially true of Internet access, a completely unsatisfying experience on the phones we tested."

David Dean, vice president and leader of The Boston Consulting Group's Technology and Communications Practice, writing on AllNetDevices.com, said "There is a big gap between what [mobile commerce] can do today and what the consumer has been led to expect." In the *New York Times*, Jeffrey Weitzen, president and CEO of Gateway, asked "Do you really need a gigahertz processor? We're finding people don't need that. The drive for speed is no longer what it once was." And Margot Suydam, writing in *commVerge* magazine, observed that "With all the hype around Bluetooth, it's no surprise that Palm has announced support for the short-range wireless standard."

Jay Salkini, president and CEO of Tecore, told *Wireless Week* that "Much hype and speculation surround next-generation networks." *Wired* magazine's "Hype List" reported that "This wireless local area network technology [Bluetooth] overcomes infrared's line-of-sight limitations, but Bluetooth's true application, much less its market potential, won't emerge until there's a critical mass of RF-chip PCs, handhelds, and phones. And even then, people looking to move data between gadgets might find it hard to sever their emotional connection to the entrenched wireline option."

In *Advertising Age*, Mohan Vishwanath, vice president of Yahoo! Everywhere, said, "As far as wireless is concerned, it's the flavor of the year. Right now, there's a lot of hype and sex appeal." And "The Explosion of Digital Markets" section of Arthur Andersen's 2000 study of technology trends stated that "Arthur Andersen's research shows that digital marketplace growth will nearly double between 2000 and 2001. This growth presents enormous opportunities for companies to profit—on both the sell-side and buy-side, but only if they can predict accurately their customer needs and develop solutions to address those needs."

What has really changed, if anything, in recent years? Certainly, we have accepted technology to the point that it has become almost transparent in our lives. We sit on the couch with the remote in hand, ready to change TV channels as rapidly as our mood changes. A cellphone or two-way messaging device has replaced the pager that used to be clipped to our belts. There's a personal digital assistant (PDA) in our shirt pocket where the calculator used to be. We're buying up millions of digital still cameras every year to replace those dowdy old-style film models. Many of us have replaced our more fashionable analog watches with multifunction digital models. We're turning entire rooms of our homes into wall-to-wall entertainment centers.

The role that technology now plays in our lives is evident from the expanded coverage it's getting in the general media and business press. Technology is news, and it is now being treated pretty much the same way the press has covered cars for so many years—with columns, features, and special advertising sections. The *Wall Street Journal* calls its weekly column "Personal Technology." The *New York Times* features a weekly section called "Circuits." Gannett newspapers carry a weekly supplement they call "e." *BusinessWeek* features a weekly Information Technology column and e-biz section. *Fortune* and *Forbes* have developed similar sections.

In fact, *Forbes* logged the biggest gain in technology coverage the third quarter of 2000, according to Sam Witmore's Media Survey, which analyzes the editorial performance of technology publications, Web sites, and broadcast outlets. *Forbes*, which specializes in financial and investment news and features, boosted its gadget coverage from 1.45 pages an issue to 5.08 pages an issue over the same period a year earlier. Whitmore says, "Increased coverage in the general business pubs is especially important because the readership they attract is different from [that of] the computing mags. The circulation of *Fortune, Forbes,* and *BusinessWeek* averages more than twice that of *InfoWorld* and *eWeek*. But you don't have access to the owner's manual until you buy the product."

It's all news, but it's not always good news, as a number of headlines published during the second half of 2000 can attest:

"Consumers Still Seem Resistant to Some New High-End Electronics"
—*New York Times*

"Mobile Devices Threaten Personal Time, Survey Finds"
—*EE Times*

"IP Cores 2001—Hype or Key to Future?"
—*Electronic News*

"Do Consumers Want Location Services?"
—*Wireless Data News*

"Wireless Data Users Dissatisfied with Service"
—*AllNetDevices.com*

"But Does Anybody Really Use This Stuff?"
—*New York Times*

Technology is hard. Design cycles keep getting shorter to get new products and new technologies to market sooner, forcing manufacturers to support overlapping design teams. Product developers constantly work at differentiating their products, only to have them copied in their competitors' next-generation product line. Fearing their engineers don't know what consumers want, some companies have begun to rely on osmosis, setting up design groups in the markets in which their newest products will be sold.

It can be a tough sell, especially if you're slow to deliver. *Vision*, the slick quarterly magazine published by the Consumer Electronics Association, wrote in its spring 2001 issue that "Technology companies, software providers and broadcasters have dangled the promise of interactive TV (iTV) for more than a decade with few concrete results to show for all the hype." And in the same issue: "The race to harness and manipulate digital audio files on a handheld player, computer and other devices became an overnight success that actually took eight years to accomplish. But its relatively recent success as a consumer electronics product, while spurred on by the Napster phenomenon and the emergence of high speed Internet access and faster and more manageable PC hardware and software, dates back to the 1980s."

"The real problem we face is not slowness in technical innovation," Lawrence Lessig, a professor at Stanford Law School who has written extensively on law and the Internet, told the *New York Times*. "The real problem is slowness in legal and civil rights innovation in response to the technological change."

Cellular phone service was launched in the United States in 1983 and it still isn't completely spread out across the country. Even where cellphone service is widely available, mostly in urban areas, it doesn't deliver as promised. Calls continue to be dropped. Voice mail messages may not be delivered for 24 hours. Billions of dollars have been spent on creating a mobile satellite communications service that is erratic at best—where it is available. Heavily promoted wireless data service using digital cellphones and other wireless devices has been slow to grow, particularly in the United States.

Then there is Bluetooth, one of the most highly hyped personal technologies in recent history. Developed as a short-range (10-meter) cable replacement for linking consumer electronics products, it becomes an "unconscious" network of an almost endless variety of applications—from ordering soft drinks out of vending machines by using a cellphone or PDA to transferring business and personal information between a cellphone in your pocket or briefcase to a laptop computer resting on a seat next to you in an airport lounge.

The vaunted Wireless Application Protocol (WAP), developed in 1997 to bring Internet content and other advanced services to digital cellular phones and other wireless devices, is a different case, but still a good example of what happens when consumers simply refuse to accept technology that doesn't work as advertised. It didn't help when industry pundits wrote articles with headlines ranging from, "*Wrong Approach to Portability*" to "*Where Are the Products?*"

Digital subscriber line, or DSL, the high-speed broadband service targeting online homes, continues to have problems. DSL has been heavily touted by regional carriers and Internet service providers as the best and fastest way to connect to the Internet, downloading 10 times faster than dial-up modems, leaving the phone line free for regular calls. But DSL companies misread the market. By the end of 2000, U.S. DSL subscribers barely topped one million, a small fraction of Internet users who apparently were unwilling to pay an additional $30 to $40 for the higher speed offered by DSL. In fairness, a few other factors account for the low numbers. DSL is only available in some areas of the United States. And customers must be within 15,000 feet of a central office—not directly, but as the wire runs. Worse, some DSL providers have simply failed to deliver promised service.

That's the short list of overhyped, where-are-they-now technologies. It gets much longer with the addition of voice recognition, Third-Generation (3G) cellular service, artificial intelligence (or AI), Internet appliances, electronic books, home networks, and high-definition television (HDTV), all of which are discussed at some length in this book.

A few of these technologies have been around for a long time, and some of these are now reinventing themselves, although slowly. Other examples topping the technology hype list are just beginning to emerge but are no less restrained in their ability to gain wide acceptance. The hype and the promise of making life easier and more productive continue to raise our expectations.

It's a promising, but tedious, process. You can have it, but not yet. Not for several months. Maybe longer. (IBM's old trick, and it worked for a long time, was to introduce, with tremendous fanfare, a line of mainframe computers a year before they were actually shipped to stave off any possibility of its customers even thinking about buying another system. As someone once said, "No one ever got fired for buying IBM.") You can get it and find out you don't really need it. Or, you get it and it doesn't work.

The *New York Times* used "Weak Reception" as the headline over a story about how slowly the wireless Internet was developing in the United States. The smaller subheadline, "U.S. Lagging Behind in Wireless, And That May Be Just As Well," undoubtedly struck a chord with anyone familiar with the technology and the market, which clearly wasn't ready for prime time.

Remember John Sculley? He was the nonengineer marketing wizard who left Pepsi to take over Apple Computer. In 1993, after months of speculation in the technical and business press, he introduced the Apple Newton MessagePad. Newton was a totally new product, and not only for the company. It represented a whole new product category. It was a very nifty-looking handheld computer designed to do a lot of neat new things, especially for a handheld device. Heavily publicized and promoted, sales ramped up quickly, but then dropped just as rapidly with total unit sales reaching about 100,000 (not a good number for a mass-market consumer electronics product) after more than a year on the market.

Reality quickly set in when Newton's reviews pointed out several shortfalls in the device's two most highly touted features—neither its handwriting recognition nor its communications systems worked as advertised. Andrew Seybold, a long-time and widely quoted industry consultant, told the *Wall Street Journal* just as Apple was beginning Newton's initial ad campaign that it was "overhyped to begin with. All I'm hearing from is disgruntled users." Even more damaging was the nationally syndicated cartoon strip "Doonesbury," which picked on the device for an entire week, focusing on its erratic performance.

AT&T didn't do much better with its EO Personal Communicator. Even though it was purchased by more than 60 corporations, it was expensive and hard to use. AT&T finally dropped the unit in early 1994, less than a year after an EO, Inc., press release said: "In an industry inundated with hype, hoopla and pie-in-the-sky promises, we are delivering on our commitment to be the first company to bring to market a personal communicator."

A similar device, called Simon, was designed by IBM and introduced by BellSouth Cellular Corp. toward the end of 1993. But it was heavy for a handheld device (18 ounces) and difficult to use; it didn't last long either. Sony introduced a similar product, the Magic Link PIC 1000, in September 1994 to compete directly with Apple's Newton. Motorola followed early in 1995 with the Envoy, a wireless communicator, and another model called Marco, which was based on Newton technology.

Apple tried to hang in, but finally stopped development of the Newton in February 1998. Eventually, designers went back to the drawing board to create a product that consumers actually wanted. The result is today's "smart phone," or PDA.

Portability is a tricky issue, which is probably why there are several magazines whose editorial focus is on helping engineers design better, small, lightweight electronic products. Wireless Internet users want and expect the same functionality and experience with their cellular phone and personal electronic organizer that they get from their more powerful, larger-screen desktop PC. They don't have it, and it's not clear that they will ever get it. Telecommunications companies are spending hundreds of millions, and in some cases billions, of dollars for new equipment and spectrum licenses in the race to develop next-generation cellular networks offering global, high-speed, Internet and data-centric services. But no one knows for sure how these services will be used, let alone how many consumers are interested in accessing the Internet anywhere, anytime from a handheld device. In fact, only 5% of the respondents to a study conducted by Allied Business Intelligence think the cellular phone will be a useful Internet access tool.

Ease-of-use continues to plague product developers. As Sony's vice president for marketing for cellular phones once told the author, "It's a phone, and everyone knows how to use a phone. They shouldn't have to come with a 150-page manual." But they do.

Nearly half of the consumers surveyed by Duracell in 1999 said they found cellphones, pagers, laptop computers, and personal digital assistants confusing to operate. Another study by Harris Online indicated that about 60% of the consumers surveyed said they have simply stopped buying the newest high-tech devices because they're too complex. Even today, 25 years after videocassette recorders were introduced, few people know how to program them.

The hype cycle—the mean time between the first exposure to the public of a technology or product and its actual acceptance in mass market terms—is getting shorter. So is the life cycle of most portable products, which have come to be treated almost as fashion items. TV sets, on the other hand, last for years. Vendors, meanwhile, continue to push high-tech products and services with features of little or limited value to consumers because of—and here's the irony—advances in the technology itself. Will they continue to buy into these advances?

"Technology's changing, consumers aren't," Nicholas G. Carr, the executive editor of *The Harvard Business Review*, wrote in one of his columns. And that's not likely to change.

You Can't Always Blame the Technology

Y *ou have to love the numbers.*
The volume of Internet traffic is doubling every 100 days. Information technology now accounts for 8% of employment in the United States, but more than 30% of the country's economic growth. The number of wireless phones is expected to surpass wired landlines by 2004. By 2005, there will probably be more than one billion wireless device users worldwide. More than 240 million people will be using their phones for wireless data exchange by the end of 2004—up from 26 million in 1999. There will be 40 million U.S.

Web subscribers by 2003, when all new cellular phones are expected to be capable of carrying voice, data, and Internet services. Worldwide digital camera shipments will top 41 million in 2004. By 2003, more people will be connected to the Web through wireless devices than through their PCs.

Some of these projections may turn out to be accurate; most of them were made by independent market research organizations and, as pointed out later in this book, their work is often easy to challenge. Unfortunately, the projections don't have to be accurate. Just by being published in hundreds of business and technical journals—often more than once—and repeated at conferences and seminars worldwide to thousands of people who then use them in their own marketing and technical presentations and strategic planning, they take on a life of their own, creating enough buzz to make them valid and actionable. They become the basis for five-year projections in business plans. Business and technology editors use the numbers to justify their article ideas; the bigger the numbers, the hotter the topic, even if they sometimes seem outrageous.

• • •

Little has changed since the National Academy of Sciences' National Research Council wrote in its 1996 study, *The Unpredictable Certainty—Information Infrastructure Through 2000*, that telecommunications industry representatives "privately acknowledge great uncertainty regarding the evolution of wireless systems." As one project reviewer noted, "The industry is growing so fast and in so many directions that few people really have a grasp of the whole." Daniel Lynch of the Interop Co. contributed to the study with his own David Letterman-style Top 10 list of "main factors" that he said would determine the outcome of the struggle to grow the Internet in a "reasonable way." Topping Lynch's list was "the media hype factor."

More recently, Chuck Macomber, who advises clients on where wireless technologies fit into their companies' business strategies, proposed in an article he wrote for *eBusiness Advisor* magazine what he called the Wireless Obsession Rationality Metric test. The WORM test, he said, would "identify and distinguish the wireless business model artifacts of hype from the truly revolutionary products." Passing the test requires giving the right answers to questions like, what makes this wireless offering so compelling that I can't wait eight hours until I access a desktop computer? And, does the wireless offering [I'm investigating] provide a timesaving service? To understand which wireless service offerings present real promise for the future, Macomber told his readers to "filter the hype and eliminate corporate spin. Apply the WORM test to the next wireless advertisement you see, and uncover the viability of that wireless value proposition."

Robbie Blinkoff, a Ph.D. anthropologist for the Context-Based Research Group, came up with pretty much the same conclusion when a consumer survey he conducted in mid-2001 found a serious gap between the actual capabilities of most wireless devices and the marketing messages about these devices provided by their vendors. The study found that terms such as "wireless Web" led users to believe they could do everything on their wireless devices they could do on their desktop PCs. Blinkoff's two key post-survey recommendations: "Don't over-promise what the devices can do, and make it easier for me to use them."

Anyone who has tried using the wireless Web has gotten the message. Microbrowsers are formatted specifically for wireless products, and they have limitations. They're designed to accommodate the very small display screens in cellular phones and personal digital assistants (PDAs). They will let you access Web pages on these and other wireless devices, but they're not the same as the browser you use in the office or at home.

The Internet was invented in 1973, but Internet telephony didn't begin to emerge as a commercial offering until 1997. And as big as it is today, we're still wringing our hands over such critical issues as "open access," taxation, privacy, security, intellectual property rights, and "smart" technologies. (You can always tell when a new or emerging technology is starting to mature or gain legitimacy: It loses its quotation marks. The same is true when some business journalists stop using the phrase "so-called" as a descriptive precursor. For example, cellular phones with integrated personal electronic organizer features are no longer referred to as "smart" phones, or "so-called" smart phones. They're now simply smart phones.)

AT&T developed the concept of cellular communications in 1947, but it took the Federal Communications Commission 28 years to allocate spectrum for cellular service and another 8 years to get cellular into limited service. Motorola showed up at FCC headquarters in April 1973 with a complete line of land mobile radio products, including a mobile cellular phone. Motorola had already built cell sites in Washington to demonstrate the new products to the FCC.

When Motorola needed a truly portable cellular phone, Martin Cooper, then Motorola's top research and development executive, set up a design contest among Motorola's industrial design team. When they completed their designs, Cooper selected the one he liked best (he took the engineer with the winning design out to dinner) and told his engineers to "fill it in" with the necessary electronics.

Cellular was slow to grow, and it wasn't helped much by a report written by the management consulting firm McKinsey & Co. for its client AT&T. McKinsey had seriously low-balled its projection of the cellphone market. In October 1983, just as cellular service was becoming commercially available in the United States (Japan actually got the jump on the United States by about a year), McKinsey told AT&T that no more than 900,000 mobile telephones would be in use in the United States by the year 2000. McKinsey's mistake (and it was a pretty big one—it was off by more than a hundred million unit sales) was that it based its projection on technology that existed at the time, a technology that produced a box of electronics that could only fit in the trunk of a car, along with a phone the size and weight of a brick. The original cellular package, per vehicle, was priced at about $3,600. Few consumers could afford it, and service was limited at the time to the metropolitan Chicago area.

Technology is hard, but it's not the only answer to getting things to market. There are other, often highly complex issues, that can have a major impact on the success or failure of new high-tech products and services. The rest of this chapter discusses some of the big ones.

Technical Standards

For anyone who has taken even a cursory interest in developing standards—also sometimes referred to as protocols and specifications—setting standards can be a very complicated and mysterious process. So much so that it can actually take years to finalize a technical standard by which an industry can develop, manufacture, and promote a product. In fact, little has changed since the U.S. Commerce Department's National Institute of Standards and Technology proclaimed at a "standards summit" in 1998 that the United States, the world's most prolific exporter of technology, was jeopardizing its leadership by not paying enough attention to the most important details of international trade, including standards.

What is a technical standard? One simple example is 35mm film. Any 35mm film will fit into any 35mm camera, no matter who makes the camera or where you buy it. (Actually, if you read the fine print on the box, 35mm film is 24 x 36mm, but we won't get into that here—35mm is still the published standard.) A less obvious example might be the nozzles at the end of the hoses used to refuel aircraft. They will fit into the fuel tank of just about any aircraft at any airport in the world.

Wireless Week accurately took the U.S. government, broadcasters, and TV set manufacturers to task in a 1998 sidebar to a feature on next-generation mobile communications ("Third Gen: What's Behind the Ballyhoo") when it noted that after years of research, advocates of some 13 different TV systems agreed on one digital technology, which required consumers to purchase new TV sets. But one year after a standard was set by the Federal Communications Commission, few HDTV sets were available. Same problem on the radio side: When it came to writing a technical standard for digital audio radio, there was only one major contender, creating a de facto standard. So selecting a standard wasn't a big issue. The outcome was that digital audio radio service was auctioned without a standard, and the key contender won the license and began building its satellite network.

Think Microsoft and you're on track in understanding the significance of a de facto standard. Your VCR is another good example. It didn't take VHS long to become the de facto global VCR standard. It isn't that VHS produced a better quality picture than Sony's Betamax. In fact, the Beta format is still the preferred standard by video professionals worldwide. But VHS got the jump on Sony with double the record/playback time (four hours) at the same price as Sony's Betamax VCR, which could only handle two hours of recording and playback. Very quickly, VHS became the de facto standard for VCRs targeted for the consumer market.

Getting a technical standard in writing for wireless local area networks, or WLAN, required more than six years of quarterly meetings, each one held in a different place in the world, most of them attended by 60 or more people from different technical backgrounds—primarily communications and computer specialists who, until recently, didn't speak the same language. And they're still at it, adding, refining, defining, and trying to keep up with changes in technology, the marketplace, and new applications.

It's complicated. A compromise proposal from Texas Instruments, Intersil Corp., and several other companies with a vested interest in the development of a WLAN standard, known as IEEE 802.11 (IEEE stands for the Institute of Electrical and Electronics Engineers; it is responsible for setting many international electrical/electronics standards), combines elements from two final independent proposals that were originally considered for what is now known as the 802.11g standard. It offers compatibility with other versions of 802.11, such as 802.11a and 802.11b. (The difference between 802.11a and 802.11b, if you must know, is that 802.11a operates in the 5 gigahertz frequency, or GHz, band, whereas 802.11b runs in the 2.4 GHz band. Each also has its limitations as to how fast it can move data through the network. The most recent proposals for 802.11g call for higher data rates—up to 54 megabits—in the 2.4 GHz band.)

The process of upgrading a standard is a moving target, with the newest versions (usually designated 1.0, then 1.1, and so forth) being published sometimes faster than companies can design and produce new products to the old standard. One of the unfortunate results of this is the introduction of a new term by standards mavens—the "du jour" standard, or the standard-of-the-day.

The Internet falls somewhere between du jour and de facto. While the Internet Engineering Task Force (IETF), the Internet's governing body, has the support of national and international standards bodies, it operates with open membership and works hard at avoiding the influence of any particular industry sector, such as computer or telecommunications groups. Where the Internet slips between the du jour and de facto cracks is that the IETF is not alone in making the Internet work. Some of the most important standards in wide use over the Internet were not developed formally through the IETF process but were proposed by others, distributed online over the Internet, and then accepted by industry without further IETF action.

Meanwhile, the cellular phones standards story is sucking up more ink and hours on the conference circuit than even the Internet. Will your cellphone work anywhere in the world? Most likely, it will not. At least, not yet. The proliferation of wireless technologies and standards has led to a patchwork of incompatible systems, often making it impossible for cellphone users to "roam" anywhere outside their home system.

Until the 1980s, the FCC played an active, if indirect, role in standards-setting, specifying technologies that licensed carriers were required to use. All cellular licensees at the time were required to use a technology called Advanced Mobile Phone Service (AMPS), which uses analog technology. Between about 1985 and 1995 the FCC withdrew from standards-setting for wireless communications, leaving it to industry to decide whether there will be a standard and what technologies will be chosen as the standard or, as it turned out, standards.

The FCC took this approach for Personal Communications Services (PCS), a mobile radio service that operates very much like cellular but is inherently digital and operates at a different frequency than cellular. Just to add to the confusion, the wireless industry began referring to PCS as "cellular, but at a different frequency," and some carriers were using "PCS" in their advertising and other promotional material when they were actually still offering only cellular.

To this day, industry groups in the United States have not settled on a single standard for digital cellular. With no consensus, there are at least three different cellular standards, which would make it difficult for subscribers to make and receive calls as they travel around the country if not for the fact that cellphone designers continue to produce phones with analog frequencies built in. When calling to a technically incompatible digital system, the phone seamlessly reverts to the old analog system. Like the VCR case, this is a pretty good (or bad, depending on where you're coming from) example of how the marketplace can set a standard. Indeed, all digital phones produced today, at least for the U.S. market, continue to provide analog (AMPS) service.

In the late 1980s, as U.S. cellular systems operators moved toward constructing digital networks, one digital technology—time division multiple access (TDMA)—emerged as the heir apparent digital cellular standard for the United States. This technology, originally developed for cellular communications by Ericsson, works by splitting a frequency channel into different time slots, producing up to a sixfold increase in channel capacity over analog cellular transmission systems. This means that up to six calls can travel over the same cellular channel.

The game suddenly changed in 1990 when San Diego-based startup Qualcomm, Inc., proposed a second technology, called code division multiple access (CDMA). Described as a U.S.-based military contractor in *Global Competitiveness of U.S. Advanced-Technology Industries: Cellular Communications*, a 1993 report on the cellular communications market published by the U.S. International Trade Commission, Qualcomm came out of almost nowhere with its CDMA-based technology which, in fact, uses a spread-spectrum technique developed originally for the U.S. military. Spread spectrum separates, or "spreads," radio signals over a wide frequency band and then reassembles these signals into a coherent transmission at the receiving end. This technique was used very successfully during World War II to make it difficult to jam or intercept radar and radio signals. It boosted the cellular network transmission capacity at least 10 times over analog systems, up to 12 to 16 times, according to Qualcomm, and had perhaps twice the channel capacity of TDMA. Just about the only CDMA equipment to be found when the ITC's report was published was in Qualcomm's own buildings and at a few demonstration sites set up by Qualcomm in San Diego to promote the technology.

However, excited by this new development, the CDMA proposal won the approval of a growing number of U.S. carriers, including those who sometimes criticized Qualcomm for its often over-the-top aggressiveness in promoting to carriers and to their lead trade association, the Cellular Telecommunications Industry Association, now the Cellular Telecommunications and Internet Association, which had already formally endorsed TDMA.

In the past, manufacturers that chose to produce equipment conforming to only one or two digital standards tended to remain niche players unless one of the standards was widely adopted, as was AMPS, the analog cellular standard in the United States. Now, with the arrival of 2.5-Generation and Third-Generation (3G) mobile technologies, the emphasis again turns to which standard or standards are best for which region.

Despite all the ink being devoted to this topic, it continues to be very confusing, at least to most consumers and even to business and professional users. Whereas most countries have pretty much settled on a single 3G standard, the United States could end up with three, making roaming between networks difficult and potentially degrading service. The argument in the United States, and one that has the support of the FCC, has always been "let the market decide." But the inevitable mixing and matching of different standards for digital cellular service in the United States is also due to the government's failure or delay in licensing new spectrum for next-generation mobile services. In fact, some of the most critical thinking among industry analysts suggests that any delay in this process is a good thing because the market simply isn't ready for next-generation wireless and that the development of competing technologies will lead to better services and more applications.

Qualcomm has done a masterful job of promoting CDMA to the industry, the media, and to regulators with an endless supply of highly readable studies and technical reports, live demonstrations, and well-organized seminars. As a result, CDMA is *the* digital cellular standard in South Korea. It is also gaining in China, the most populous cellphone user base in the world, and it is one of the key digital standards in the United States. CDMA was projected to account for more than 75 million cellphone sales worldwide in 2001.

Qualcomm's efforts in promoting CDMA in the 3G standards wars will be absolutely critical. The Geneva-based International Telecommunications Union (ITU), an agency of the United Nations, has endorsed CDMA20001xEV-DO, a CDMA 3G protocol. This standard is fully compatible with all proposed 3G equipment and services. It gives Qualcomm full certification for 3G, whereas GSM, despite the fact that it dominates the digital cellular world in terms of total cellphone population, has won only partial ITU approval.

Bluetooth is another good/bad example of how heavy-handed hype can significantly impact a market. Named after a 10th century Nordic king, this is the short-range, low-power wireless link that operates unconsciously between just about any wireless device that is Bluetooth-enabled. Despite huge expectations and the promise of a flood of new Bluetooth-equipped wireless devices in 2000, Bluetooth-based devices are just now coming to market, although so far mainly in the form of accessories, such as headsets for hands-free cellphone use. Even futuristic applications, which have become the source of so much of the Bluetooth hype, are meaningless until there is a significant enough user base to support them. My Bluetooth-based cellphone or PDA can't communicate with your cellphone or PDA if it isn't Bluetooth-enabled.

Who's to blame for all the noise about Bluetooth? Certainly the technical and business press, which has been covering its long-awaited development from day one. But much of it also rests on the strong shoulders of the more than 2,000 company members in the Bluetooth Special Interest Group (SIG), all trying to get their names out into the ether as quickly as possible as a "Bluetooth vendor." At one point, more than 250 devices were listed on the SIG Web site, but many of these were demonstration products and were not "qualified"—in other words, they did not yet meet the SIG's own technical specifications, or standards. That began to change with the availability of commercial Bluetooth chips, and by early 2002, more than 500 Bluetooth-enabled devices had been "certified" by the SIG. Still, literally hundreds of thousands of words were devoted to Bluetooth during 2001, helped along by the launch of *Bluetooth World*, a magazine dedicated to the technology.

One of the realities in technology development is that product design cycles are becoming shorter, forever growing consumer expectations for each new generation of products. New portable devices must be smaller, with batteries that last at least as long as their service contracts, and they must be loaded with lots of new features. This is not a very good environment for the historically plodding standards-setting process.

At least one organization has taken this to heart. In 1999, the IEEE, the largest technical society in the world with more than 350,000 members, formed the IEEE Industry Standards and Technology Organization (IEEE-ISTO) to more fully address industry standards. Intended to complement the existing IEEE Standards Association, the IEEE-ISTO said at the outset that it would provide a forum for industry groups to develop specifications that meet rapid product schedules. Since then, other major industry groups, such as the International Telecommunications Union (ITU), have vowed to enhance their specifications to improve the performance of next-generation wireless communications. The trick for the ITU will be to harmonize global wireless services while maintaining the relevancy of local market needs.

Writing standards is a daunting task, particularly given the rapid rate of the introduction of new technology-based products.

Bureaucracy

There hardly ever is a shortage of bureaucratic screw-ups that slow the development or improvement of just about anything, certainly not where technology is involved. There always seems to be some little behind-the-scenes thing or person underlying the hype with the potential to bring everything to a screeching halt. One of the more timely examples is the ongoing effort to keep pace with the growth of the Internet.

The Internet was designed to handle a total of about 4.3 billion computers and related devices. That was a big number 20 years ago. But with the prospect of a lot more devices being tied into the Internet—everything from cellular phones to cable television boxes, utility meters, automobiles, and even home appliances—experts expect the network to max out in less than five years. The problem is, there are not enough addresses in the current system to support the network's growth and new applications.

In anticipation of continued growth over the next several years, engineers are working on a number of innovative techniques. One is to upgrade the system, known as Internet version 4, or IPv4, to IPv6. (There was an IPv5, but it was experimental.) Initially, anyone could continue to use IPv4, which technically could operate alongside IPv6. But IPv6 isn't expected to be able to work seamlessly with IPv4 until at least 2006 and may not be ready to completely take over for IPv4 until 2010.

The battle over how to handle this issue rages within the Internet Engineering Task Force (IETF), the body that oversees the Internet. IPv6 supporters insist that IPv6 is needed because the Internet is simply running out of numeric IP addresses, most of which were scooped up early in the United States, leaving a drought abroad. It hasn't helped that Stanford University and the Massachusetts Institute of Technology each received blocks of 16 million IP addresses which, according to analysts at the Gartner Group, is more than all of the Internet addresses assigned to China.

Critics of the upgrade question whether the address numbers will grow as rapidly as many product designers hope.

They probably will if products such as the next generation of camcorders are linked to the manufacturer to monitor their performance or if home appliances are tied into the Internet, as eventually expected. Again, the question becomes, how many consumers really need, or even want, this feature?

While the IPv6 debate rages on, Internet service providers have had to resort to some technical tricks to ensure that their subscribers don't run out of addresses. One is to use a network address translator, essentially a gateway that enables multiple devices to share the same number. The problem with this solution is that it may not support interactive services; in other words, one of the players of an Internet-based game may not be able to find the other players connected through the translator.

A much more complicated, and potentially painful, example of bureaucratic fumbling came out of the 1993 New York World Trade Center terrorist bombing when federal agencies (FBI, U.S. Secret Service, the military) and local law enforcement, fire departments, and ambulance services could not communicate. Each agency has its own set of radio frequencies assigned to it by the Federal Communications Commission. In the hours and days following the bombing, they could not talk to each other directly from any remote location. A fireman on one of the upper floors in the twin towers of the World Trade Center could not quickly and efficiently communicate with an emergency medical crew on the ground. The NYPD could not talk to the FBI.

What came out of that experience was the formation of the Public Safety Wireless Advisory Committee. Manned with representatives from several federal agencies, the committee spent a year looking at issues ranging from frequency assignments to available and emerging technologies before turning out a 600-page report that was loaded with background information, operational data, and even several conclusions. But nothing has changed. As one program manager put it in an interview in the July 2001 issue of *Portable Design* magazine, "There was no one agency that could follow up on this. Everyone has their own requirements."

On October 11, 2001, exactly one month after the September 11 terrorist attacks on the World Trade Center and the

Pentagon, Richard Clarke, appointed the president's cyber-space security advisor only a week earlier, told the *Washington Post* that emergency workers should have priority access to wireless communications during crises, in part because they could not place wireless calls after the September 11 attacks. National security officials, firefighters, and other emergency services personnel could not communicate when wireless carriers were suddenly swamped with calls. "It is essential," Clarke told the *Post*, "that we work with industry to deploy priority access service for use in crisis situations as soon as possible." It didn't help that the National Communications System (formerly the Emergency Broadcast System), an umbrella organization of federal government agency communications specialists, established in the early 1960s, was located in the World Trade Center. (In July 2000, the FCC said that while it would allow, but not require, cellular phone carriers to give priority access to federal, state, and local emergency workers to cover national security and emergency needs, there are no plans to tie wireless users into the National Communications System.) Within days of Clarke's appointment, the White House asked the Cellular Telecommunications and Internet Association (CTIA), the cellular communications industry's lead trade association, what it could do in the short term to give government agencies priority access to the nation's wireless networks, similar to a system that already exists for traditional wired phone lines.

It's technically complicated. For one thing, unlike wired phone systems, there is no dedicated link between a cellular phone and a telephone switching center. But the CTIA and others, including emergency services specialists, worry that giving priority status to federal agencies, even in a crisis, would deprive regular wireless subscribers access to 911 assistance in emergencies.

Not surprisingly, the terrorist attacks now have European wireless carriers thinking about how they might enhance their network capacity to better handle high-volume voice and data traffic in emergencies. One possibility is that the events of September 11 may prompt American consumers to start thinking more about using short text messaging to communicate instead of voice, especially when voice service is not immediately available. Short messaging, which is very popular in Europe and Japan, is only beginning to make a dent in the United States, in part because you can send a message only to someone with the same wireless carrier. This will likely change over the next few years, partly as a result of a strong nudge from the FCC and partly as U.S. carriers upgrade their networks.

Convergence

Convergence is one of those amorphous areas that often plays a key role in the hype cycle, but it is an area that few understand, whether you're talking about social convergence, global convergence, or technical convergence, which the MIT Media Lab's Nicholas Negroponte calls the transformation of atoms to bits. But even in a technology context, it's also a marketing concept and a cultural issue to the extent that it seems to be widely accepted just about everywhere but the United States.

Convergence means different things to different people, but in the technical community it usually refers to integrating technologies and applications that once were separate, such as communications and computers. For example, integrating a cellphone and PDA in the same device is convergence.

One industry-supplied definition is, "The act of bringing the Internet to devices that previously couldn't access it. This could include the merging of the Internet with television, cellular phones, or even kitchen appliances." Microsoft's Bill Gates doesn't like this definition. He believes that convergence is not about moving to a single device, but much more about linking devices through software. Microsoft's vision is to "connect everything" through a universal plug-and-play specification that uses the Internet to link practically every household appliance, PC, and home entertainment system. From a practical point of view, anyone could meet just about all of their personal communications and mobile computing needs with a cellphone, a PDA, a two-way pager (or other type of messaging device), and a digital camera, but then they might also have to carry a miniature digital recorder to remind them not to forget to carry all this stuff.

The graphical pies that represent the marketing positions of telecommunications, computing, and consumer electronics in PowerPoint presentations given in one seminar and business meeting after another were already beginning to overlap in 1996 when Stuart Lipoff, an analyst with Arthur D. Little, Inc., and the president of the IEEE Consumer Electronics Society (he's now a partner at Applied Value Corp.), suggested that while the consumer electronics industry has focused primarily on entertainment, this technology-driven market was now moving to information and communications. "The mode of use," he said at the time, "is moving from one-way passive to two-way interactive."

The Dick Tracy-like wrist cellphones are here. National Semiconductor's Origami Mobile Communicator goes even further, combining a phone and wireless video with a digital camera, MP3 audio, PDA, Internet access, e-mail, and Microsoft Windows XP operating system into a 7.5-inch long, 4-inch wide, 1.5-inch thick unit weighing about 10 ounces. It uses a Bluetooth-equipped access point, with a built-in wide-area network with two digital transmission standards (GSM and CDMA), ensuring that it can be used just about anywhere in the world. National's Origami pitch: "Multifunction or convergence products tend to be a bargain versus several single-function products, and they take up less space."

Adding wireless communications to a PDA, such as a Palm or Pocket PC, is a relatively simple, if not very elegant, example. Nokia's 5510 is a mobile phone with e-mail, an FM radio, video game player, music player (which can be recorded from CDs), and a text messenger, a QWERTY-style keyboard, and a headphone jack. Handspring's Treo is a cellphone, PDA, and a BlackBerry-style, two-way text messaging device all in one.

Everyone with a serious interest in wireless is hoping that Bluetooth lives up to the Cahners In-Stat Group's prediction that Bluetooth-enabled equipment will grow at a compounded annual rate of 360% between 2001 and 2005. That translates to 955 million Bluetooth devices shipped in 2005. But, like so many other "hot" new features, how many people will actually use the Bluetooth feature, even after they try it a few times?

At its most practical level, the Swiss Army knife approach to developing new products is often the result of product designers attempting to add value to an existing product or product line or to differentiate an existing products from a competitor's line simply by adding new features to that product. Or to try to satisfy a particular market segment or customer. (There are still a few TV/radio combo units in hotel and motel rooms, but these too are disappearing.)

Actually, manufacturers are becoming very creative about what they put in the same box.

Sony and others are taking convergence to a new level with the introduction of digital cellphones that allow you to check e-mail, access the Internet, listen to recorded music, check calendars, weather reports, sports scores, stock quotes, and news headlines, and play games. Palm now offers several snap-on attachments for its PDAs, including a digital camera and a Global Positioning System (GPS) device as a navigational aid. Matsushita, Thomson, Philips, and Sony now market personal video recorders with hard drives that can record up to 30 hours of TV programming.

The convergence phenomena has even been studied by the Office of Technology Assessment, an agency of the U.S. Congress. In a 300-page report, *Wireless Technologies and the National Information Infrastructure*, published in 1995, the OTA separates convergence into three distinct scenarios:

One is *convergence technology*, where computer power and communications technologies are integrated to improve functionality and offer new applications. For example, the marriage of computer power and radio technology was crucial in the development of cellular radio. Computers route calls to the correct cells and handle handoffs as mobile users move from one cell to another. The networks that allow cellular users to roam are actually interconnected computer databases.

Another is the *convergence of applications*, where voice, data, and video services can be offered over the same network. Today, networks of all kinds—whether originally developed to transmit voice, data, or video—are being improved in order to carry all kinds of information in many different combinations. Cellular service providers have begun to offer a wider range of data services, and some of the new low-early orbit (LEO) mobile satellite systems are designed to carry both voice and data.

Finally, there is the *convergence of networks and companies* through mergers, acquisitions, and joint ventures. An obvious example is the acquisition of McCaw Cellular by AT&T. This type of convergence called for the merger of a combination of systems, including AT&T's long-distance network and McCaw Cellular's local system.

The digital marketplace is projected to nearly double its growth every year over the next few years, but Accenture (formerly Andersen Consulting) says that will occur only if companies can accurately predict their customers needs and develop solutions to address those needs. One of the most important elements to future success, suggests Accenture, is to accurately read consumers' appetite for product integration. Is convergence a good thing? The technology is impressive but, again, how many people need, or will actually use, most of these features?

Not many, according to research by Arthur D. Little, which says its research indicates that almost two-thirds of respondents to its survey prefer using specialized devices rather than a single all-in-one device. Lucent Technologies is conducting its own research into this issue and is spending $10 million to study the impact of convergence of technologies on people who are living in an increasingly mobile economy.

Interoperability

Except for some technical trickery to make interoperability seemingly transparent to cellular phone users, virtually every new and emerging wireless communications development has a compatibility problem. The cellphone you're using, for example, operates in different parts of the country, or the world, only because it has chips that accommodate different technical standards in each of those areas.

Although conceived simply as a cable replacement for the unseemly nest of wires that connects PCs to keyboards and printers, Bluetooth quickly evolved into a short-range (initially up to 30 feet) wireless network that will allow people to "unconsciously" detect and communicate with each other through a variety of mainly portable devices without user intervention. Bluetooth-enabled devices can "talk" to each other as they come into range and send e-mail from a PDA or a laptop computer to the cellular phone in a nearby briefcase. Or images can be downloaded from a Bluetooth-equipped digital camera to a PC or cellphone. But Bluetooth has had interoperability problems almost from the beginning (that would be 1994).

Until well into 2001, few Bluetooth-enabled products had been tested under actual user conditions. Under the rules set by the Bluetooth Special Interest Group, the umbrella organization that essentially monitors and regulates the technology, products must be tested at a qualified test facility to ensure compliance with the Bluetooth technical specification. Only a few of these qualification test facilities were listed on the official Bluetooth Web site going into 2001, when the industry and market research firms were projecting new Bluetooth-based products would be hitting retailer shelves.

A heavily promoted product demonstration at the 2001 European CeBit, one of the biggest and best-attended high-tech trade shows in the world, failed to demonstrate the most important element in Bluetooth's functionality—its compatibility with other Bluetooth devices—sparking rumors that Bluetooth still could not work out of the box. Microsoft's decision not to support Bluetooth in its XP operating system didn't help.

Some easier-to-use Bluetooth products, such as PC cards, adapters, and a headset, began to appear in 2001. But market research organizations who were burned by their own overzealous projections were becoming very cautious about making any long-term market estimates. In 1999, for example, The Meta Group said the ubiquitous use of Bluetooth would be obvious in 2002. A year later, the market research firm says this won't happen until at least 2004. Even Ericsson, which invented Bluetooth, admitted that it will take more time to hit the big numbers as vendors struggled to get enough Bluetooth-enabled devices into the market to test (or prove) their interoperability in the real world.

Several companies, including AT&T Wireless, Cingular Wireless, MM02, NTT DoCoMo, Telefonica Moviles, Vodafone, Fujitsu, Matsushita Electric, Mitsubishi Electric, Motorola, NEC, Nokia, Samsung, Sharp, Siemens, Sony, Ericsson, Toshiba, and Symbian, have launched an initiative to introduce interoperable mobile Internet access and visual content downloading services worldwide for next-generation wireless services. Their goal is to create a true global mass market with the development of an open mobile services architecture.

Nokia and Sony are also now working together to ensure interoperability between mobile handsets and other consumer devices by different manufacturers through the development of an open and common middleware software platform. NTT DoCoMo and Nokia have also joined forces to promote an open mobile architecture for next-generation wideband-CDMA services and will make the results of their cooperative effort available to the wireless industry to ensure that their products communicate with each other.

Regulatory Issues

Technological innovations have been coming so thick and fast for so long that they have exceeded governments' ability to regulate them. This is particularly true for the telecommunications industry where just one issue, the allocation of spectrum for wireless services, has become a political fiasco that eventually involved the White House and publicly pitted several agencies, including the Pentagon and the Commerce Department, against each other.

After months of battling with the Federal Communications Commission and the National Telecommunications and Information Administration (NTIA), the U.S. Commerce Department agency that oversees government agencies' use of the airwaves, the Pentagon refused to give up any of the vast swath of radio frequencies it uses for everything from communications to radar and weapons control. Commercial broadcasters, meanwhile, continue to lobby for more spectrum and, unlike wireless carriers, who have been paying for the use of "airwaves" through FCC-sponsored auctions, broadcasters want it free. And they usually get it from a cooperative Congress. In fact, the FCC generally goes along with whatever Congress and the White House want, as does the NTIA.

Government regulation initially stemmed from the perception that telecommunications is a public good, offering economic and social benefits to the public beyond those delivered directly to individual consumers. But as the U.S. International Trade Commission (ITC) pointed out in one of its many studies nearly 10 years ago, the availability of new communication technologies, such as cellular, has led many governments, including the United States, to modify their regulatory frameworks. In the United States, competitive service provision has been preferable to monopoly for a long time—at least since the breakup of AT&T—to the extent that it is expected to increase service quality and reduce prices. This is certainly true for cellular communications.

In addition to boosting competition, cellular has raised other issues with some regulators, mainly those related to network interconnection and standards-setting. Other developments, such as spectrum allocation, are more specific to cellular and other wireless services and, therefore, receive a lot more ink. The treatment of these, as the ITC has pointed out, has created a fluid regulatory environment, requiring an ongoing discussion of key regulatory issues. Meanwhile, the Administration says it has a "new plan" to divide up the airwaves to make room for next-generation wireless services. While the wireless industry is pushing the development of new services based on fast-emerging technologies, the federal government's plan involves a two-year delay to auction spectrum for these services. Part of the delay is the result of the terrorist attacks on the World Trade Center and the Pentagon and a reassessment of requirements for future military operations.

The real question is, "Is there enough spectrum to accommodate the fast-growing number of cellphone subscribers in the United States, particularly when current users upgrade to Third-Generation (3G) phones when they become available?" Despite the hype, not yet.

Under an order signed by President Clinton, the United States reviewed its spectrum allocation policy for new wireless services and was scheduled to conduct a major auction to award new licenses for 3G services beginning in September 2002. Clinton's involvement follows the publication of a report published by the White House Council of Economic Advisers that concluded that two areas most affected by the order—wireless communications and the Internet—have been key elements in the nation's productivity and economic improvements and that it is vital to continue their development. Also, the United States does not want to fall behind the rest of the world in these two areas—both of which it more or less invented.

TRUE STORY

Some years ago, I attended a late afternoon reception in one of those very large, ornate rooms at one of Washington's posh midtown hotels following a day-long telecom conference when I spotted a familiar face across the crowded room. It was Richard Wiley, the chairman of the Federal Communications Commission. He was standing by himself, drink in hand, sort of taking in the crowd. As the communications editor of *Electronic News* at the time (by far, the hottest publication in the industry in those days), I thought it would be a great opportunity to introduce myself personally to Wiley and maybe get in a few questions, hopefully without making it sound like an interview.

Slightly intimidated despite years of interviewing important industry leaders and even politicians, I thought I would start the conversation with something kind of innocuous. After introducing myself, I suggested to Wiley, a prominent telecom lawyer even before being named chairman of the FCC, that given the rapid development and complexity of the technology, wouldn't it make more sense for the commission chairmanship to be held by an engineer, not a lawyer? Wiley had to think about that for just about a nanosecond before responding with a very emphatic "NO!"

Legislation

New technologies often require new laws to govern them. Unfortunately, these laws often fall short of the mark, either because they are so watered down as to be nearly meaningless or because they are immediately challenged, significantly slowing their effectiveness. Or, in some awkward form of reverse hype, the people who wrote them simply don't understand the dynamics of the technologies or the market that must eventually support them. Then, of course, there's the possibility that the technology is advancing so fast that any new law is out of date when it hits the books. Broadband deployment, electronic privacy, intellectual property (Napster et al.), electronic commerce, cyber-terrorism, the wireless Internet, energy standards, and making room for digital television are pretty good examples of the problem.

Somehow, the United States has managed to survive and even prosper for nearly 62 years with the Communications Act of 1934, a stretch of time that saw some of the most dramatic technological and political developments in history, including the breakup of AT&T's monopoly status, the introduction of wireless communications to the masses, and, of course, the Internet.

Finally convinced that new legislation might be necessary to deal with the world as we know it today, Congress passed the Telecommunications Act of 1996. This was legislation that was intended primarily to eliminate years of stifling regulation and create a more competitive environment. One of its key goals was to break up local phone company monopolies, promising more choices in local phone services, better quality, lower rates, and easy access to high-speed Internet services.

The Telecom Act hasn't lived up to its promise. Nearly six years after its passage, there seems to be little to show for the high-level buzz that went into this legislation. Consumer complaints continue to rise and local phone rates are still high. Carriers have become favorite targets of TV and radio consumer advocate reporters, warning us about the built-in "extra" charges and the fine print in our phone bills. Only about 10% of U.S. consumers have any meaningful choice in their phone services. With the exception of cellular service, where more than half of the subscribers in the United States change their carrier every two years, barely 3% have switched wireline carriers. No sooner had the new law been passed than the local Bells went to court to challenge it, tying it up for more than two years. The U.S. Supreme Court finally upheld the Telecom Act of 1996, but local telecom carriers continue to challenge the law, mainly over provisions covering how they can price access to their local networks.

With all the pushing and shoving between the telecom carriers and consumer protection organizations, Congress is now thinking about rewriting at least parts of the Telecom Act of 1996 or even throwing it out altogether and starting from scratch to produce a set of laws that truly address today's regulatory climate and technologies. But with everything else on Congress' political plate, that's not likely to happen anytime soon.

Not surprisingly, most new telecom-related legislation is targeted at the Internet as Congress continues to wrestle with who can access the Internet—and how. The most contentious of these is the Tauzin-Dingell bill, named after its key sponsors. Telecommunications companies spent upwards of $5 million in political contributions on this legislation, the "big bucks bill of the year," surpassing, according to the *New York Times*, the fight over a patients' bill of rights. The measure, aimed at deregulating the high-speed Internet market, has the regional Bell companies—such as Verizon, SBC Communications, and BellSouth—on one side, hoping to eliminate restrictions of the Telecom Act of 1996, and the long-distance carriers, like AT&T and Sprint, on the other side, trying to win Congressional favor for sticking to current rules lest the regionals, already strong in their own communities, cut too deeply into their long-distance revenues. "Do we really want to put back together what Judge Green tore apart?" U.S. Rep. Conrad Burns (R-MT) asked a trade show audience in January 2002, a reference to the breakup of the Bell monopoly. Lots of other people, including market analysts and consumer groups, also oppose the legislation.

Other bills introduced in the U.S. House and Senate in 2001 include two different Unsolicited Commerce Electronic Mail Acts (HR 718 and HR 95), the Anti-Spamming Act (HR 1017), the Wireless Telephone Spam Protection Act (HR 113), and the Controlling the Assault of Non-Solicited Pornography and Marketing Act (S 630) which, among its many other features, requires the sender to honor opt-out requests.

Although satellites and wireless systems have grown dramatically in recent years, cable modems and digital subscriber lines, or DSLs, are winning the battle for broadband access to the Internet virtually worldwide. Barely four years ago, few homes in the United States could access the Internet by DSL or cable. DSL lines in service in North America totaled 5,509,386 at the end of 2001, or an increase of 542,206 subscribers over the end of the third quarter, according to data collected by TeleChoice, Inc. Canada exceeded a million DSL lines by the end of 2001.

Rather than promote wireless access to the Internet, most legislation before Congress has sought to restrict it, particularly when it comes to requiring Web retailers to enable consumers to "opt out" of having their data sold or used in any way. The Consumer Internet Privacy Enhancement Act (HR 237), for example, is designed to prevent Web sites from collecting personal information without prior notification of what is being collected and how it is being used. The proposed Location Privacy Protection Act before the U.S. Senate requires companies that provide wireless location-based services to notify users they are collecting information about their location. The Electronic Rights for the 21st Century Act (S 854) is designed to increase consumers' privacy for information collected over the Internet, such as the programs they watch over satellite TV systems and what books they purchase online. There are also a slew of Internet tax bills before Congress that cover the sales of Internet-based catalog houses and other so-called remote selling.

Is there a clearer example of the impact of technology on the law and new legislation than the spate of local, state, and even proposed federal legislation aimed at forcing people to stop using their cellular phones while driving? New York was the first state in the country to pass a law banning handheld cellphone use while driving, but as of November 2001, similar legislation was pending in 42 other states, all of which will lead to the growth of sales of accessories designed specifically to accommodate "hands free" mobile calls. Oregon and Oklahoma have done a complete flip on the issue, prohibiting municipalities in these states from banning the phones in vehicles.

Apparently, reading maps (paper or video-displayed GPS) and newspapers while driving is okay. So is watching TV, eating, writing, playing with the radio, applying makeup, and sorting through CDs. How will legislators respond when just about everyone on the road has e-mail and Internet access? Or when they start playing with their new 100-channel satellite radio, dash-mounted DVDs, MP3 changers, in-dash CD players, and in-vehicle interactive video with downloadable games? All in one vehicle.

TRUE STORY

In the early 1930s, McGraw-Hill's *Electronics*, the first magazine published specifically for the electronics industry, editorialized that motorists would not be able to drive and listen to the radio at the same time.

Mergers and Alliances

The acquisition binge is ongoing, particularly among telecommunications operators and manufacturers, but *Dial M for Mobile*, a study by Roland Berger Strategy Consultants in cooperation with the New York Media Association, suggests that we're only now seeing the tip of the iceberg. "Wireless," says Katherine Pendill, the study's coauthor, "is more than just hype. It really is the new big thing." Pendill believes that over the next few years, wireless communications will turn all U.S. industries and business processes upside down, adding mobile commerce (or m-commerce, the mobile equivalent of electronic, or e-commerce) functionality and advertising supported wireless entertainment—even improving companies' supply chain management.

Significantly, the technology is not coming from the United States and spreading to Europe and Asia as it often does; it's everywhere at once. Technology companies have always merged with and acquired other companies to gain market share and access to needed technologies. Speed-to-market is critical, according to a Berger/NYMA study, and with the current shattering of the wireless Internet value chain, all players—wireless operators, software providers, portals, and handset manufacturers—are moving quickly to secure a dominant position. Companies continue to believe that by partnering on a global level, they can acquire much needed technologies and other capabilities that will speed their products and services to market.

Hewlett-Packard wanted to acquire Compaq. Walter B. Hewlett, son of the cofounder of HP, William Hewlett, and an HP board member, didn't like the idea, creating one of the most heated and publicized proxy fights in recent history.

Hewlett claimed the deal was too costly and too risky and that HP should stick to what it knows best and not merge with a company whose core product is low-margin personal computers. "Do not trade HP's crown jewel imaging and printing business for Compaq's low-margin commodity computing business," Hewlett wrote in a full-page ad in the *New York Times*, hoping to sway HP stockholders his way. Carleton S. Fiorina, HP's CEO, who was leading the merger charge, told hundreds of Wall Street analysts and investors in a New York presentation a few weeks before the proxy note not to listen to the "noise" (newspaper ads, press releases, and mass mailings). Although agreeing that many high-tech mergers don't work, she called Hewlett's gripes about the merger "a press release, not a plan."

Does the hype pay? It apparently did for the winner of this months-long battle and for the *Times*, the *Wall Street Journal*, and a few other financial publications, which ran full-page ads paid for either by HP or Walter Hewlett and his group almost daily.

Investments

Wireless service providers have already spent billions of dollars to upgrade their services. Intel estimates that cellular carriers have spent more than $120 billion acquiring spectrum through FCC-sponsored auctions and will have to shell out another $180 billion to upgrade their network equipment for next-generation services.

In Europe, six German and five British telecom companies have already agreed to pay more than $80 billion for new licenses; network operators in other European countries expect to pay similar amounts to develop their next-generation services.

In the United States, under the law, if any incumbent tele-communications service (such as spectrum assigned to law enforcement agencies) has to move to make room for new services, the new carrier must finance the incumbents' move. And then there are the literally hundreds of millions of dollars required to develop new technologies for new products and services.

This is not hype. Even the often cynical trade and business press, which has its own stake in the success of future developments in wireless communications, continues to ask questions like "How many people really need the level of technical sophistication made possible by 3G services?"

Wireless growth has been spectacular, but even the most optimistic projections by industry leaders cannot be sustained. After climbing rapidly to a 54% annual growth rate worldwide, growth levels for the global cellular subscriber market are expected to slow significantly through 2007, especially in mature markets. This does not bode well for anyone pitching the wireless Internet. Despite lowering expectations for the United States and Europe, total worldwide PC shipments are expected to grow about 17% annually and will remain the dominant means of accessing the Internet—at least until consumers begin to take more seriously the information appliances, including Internet-connected TVs, consumer network computers, Web tablets, e-mail-only devices, personal digital assistants (PDAs), Internet-enabled mobile phones, and Internet game consoles.

The VC Market

The venture capital (VC) picture began fading along with the New Economy, making it harder for startups to get funding. After surveying its 400 member firms about the state of the VC market in the summer of 2001, the National Venture Capital Association (NVCA) reported that New Economy markets are "preparing for an extremely difficult economic environment over the next 12 to 18 months." This is in sharp contrast to earlier experience when the amount of VC invested in U.S. companies jumped from more than $17 billion in 1997 to nearly $104 billion in the late 1990s.

Venture capitalists signed checks for nearly $3 billion into 180 telecom startups in 2001 in the United States, a big drop from the $7.5 billion they laid out for 365 companies in just the first half of 2000. Most of this growth came out of the dot-com boom when VCs were rumored to be signing checks for dot-com startups, based on 20-minute presentations that included the skimpiest of business plans. As one VC manager put it, "There's a discipline that got lost in the Internet and e-commerce hype."

It's a rough ride. Broadband companies pulled in $27.5 million in VC money in one week in December 2001, but that was down from the $54.4 million they collected a week earlier and the $72.7 million a week before that. VC funding for wireless companies grew only 1% from the third quarter to the fourth quarter in 2001 and would have been down 17%, according to Rutberg & Co., a financial research firm, without $346 million funded to Vesper, a Brazilian network, and the $155 million to Star 21, a German company. The funding for wireless-related concerns would have been even smaller if not for investments from less traditional investors, such as Nokia Venture Partners, One Motorola Ventures, Lucent Venture Partners, Ericsson Venture Partners, and the VC arms of Intel, Qualcomm, Texas Instruments, Kyocera Wireless, Microsoft, and Siemens AG. The VC dollars sent to software companies was more than halved in the first three quarters of 2001 compared to the previous year.

As a key player in the hype cycle, VCs have taken some heat in the technology press in terms usually applied to lawyers and used car salesmen. David Bunnell, editorial director of UMAC, Inc., describes a fictitious conversation in the September 2001 issue of *UPSIDE* magazine between a VC and a group of startup hopefuls who just flew in to San Jose from St. Louis looking for funding. "You're putting too much quality into your products," the VC says. "We need higher margins and a stronger bottom line." Later in the meeting the VC tells them, "Of course, we'll want 85% of your company and seven out of eight board seats. But that's generous by today's standards."

VCs also took a beating in an essay in the September 2001 issue of *IEEE Spectrum,* headlined "An Engineer's View of Venture Capitalists." Written by Nick Tredennick and Brion Shimamoto of Dynamic Silicon, it suggests that engineers are being shortchanged by professional investors. "VCs know how to deal with engineers, but engineers don't know how to deal with VCs," they write. "VCs take advantage of this situation to maximize the return for the venture fund's investors." A suggestion by Tredennick and Shimamoto: "Don't send [a VC] your business plan unless the VC has personally requested it." Also, "VCs are sheep and the electronics industry is driven by fads, just as the fashion and toy industries are. If one big-name VC firm funds reconfigurable electronic blanket weavers, the others follow."

Nevertheless, VC activity was down in the first quarter of 2001 with the number of new VC funds receiving new capital from their (mainly institutional) investors dropping from 147 in the previous year's comparable period to 95. The result is that VCs are doing more due diligence and are less susceptible to hype, which means they are seeking less risky ventures and being very cautious about more speculative investments.

Litigation

Suing Microsoft and the Napster people may have slowed them slightly, but any technology that works, is relatively easy to use, and is cheap (better yet, free), will attract attention, lawyers and other special interests notwithstanding.

Jack Valenti found this out the hard way. Scared to death that new-fangled VCRs posed a serious threat to the motion picture industry, the president of the Motion Picture Association of America and former top aide to Lyndon Johnson told Congress in 1982, "The growing and dangerous intrusion of this new technology threatens an entire industry's economic vitality and future security."

The popcorn hit the fan when the MPAA took its case to the U.S. Supreme Court. But it couldn't stop this new technology that was already in hundreds of thousands of homes. With hundreds of millions of VCRs sold since then, video rental income now rivals movie box-office receipts. Fear and the consumer electronics industries' hype aside, VCRs have not replaced movies any more than radio killed newspapers (except, perhaps, for those very few and far between "Extra" editions), TV destroyed radio, cable TV killed the movies, or digital cameras replaced film.

In a case all too reminiscent of the hundreds of millions of dollars spent fighting Big Tobacco and the asbestos industry, plaintiffs and lawyers are trying to make more big bucks from cellular phone manufacturers, carriers, and the industry's trade association, claiming their products are dangerous to your health. This, despite the fact that millions have already been spent researching this issue with no clear evidence that radio frequency emissions are a health hazard.

One of these wireless companies, Qualcomm, ran into another kind of legal buzzsaw when it began to put a serious dent in an already mature and widely accepted digital cellular technology with CDMA, a technology it pioneered and essentially owns.

CDMA, or code division multiple access, is based on a concept known as frequency hopping in which radio signals are randomly transmitted over different frequencies and then merged at the receiving end into a coherent signal or message. The technology was developed originally to avoid jamming radio-controlled torpedoes and eavesdropping on military communications. (The original patent for this "spread spectrum" radio transmission technique was issued to Hollywood actress Hedy Lamarr and composer/concert pianist George Antheil in 1942, but that's another story.) CDMA's big advantage over other digital cellular systems, which it pounded away at with trade association officials, regulators, the editors of industry publications, and in live demonstrations for wireless network carriers is that it offers several more channels than competing technologies and therefore can better and more economically handle more voice and data traffic.

In the fall of 1996, Qualcomm was having problems delivering CDMA-based handsets—mainly, it said, because of slow component deliveries. The *Wall Street Journal* jumped on the company with a highly critical, page-one story, suggesting that some of the biggest names in telecommunications had invested as much as $20 billion based on promises about CDMA technology made by Qualcomm founder, chairman, and CEO Irwin Jacobs. Jacobs immediately wrote a letter to the *WSJ* that was never published, arguing that companies "do not rely on anyone's hype" when making critical decisions.

But they do, certainly in Qualcomm's case. It was only Qualcomm's soon-to-be legendary promotional and marketing skills that turned it into the multibillion dollar success that it is today. CDMA is now a major force in cellular telecommunications and has been widely accepted around the world. Although most of Europe continues to use a different technology, known as GSM (for Global System for Mobile Communications), CDMA is poised to become the baseline technology for next-generation wireless services worldwide.

TRUE STORY

Every once in awhile, someone comes up with a can't-miss idea that never makes it to market, often for reasons beyond anyone's control. Here's an unusual, but true, example:

The people who designed TV sets for RCA Consumer Electronics about 20 or so years ago decided that it was time to literally go "outside the box" and do something about the utterly staid and boring look of its products. After all, it is a box—usually with a metal or veneer wood finish designed to fit a specific-size cathode ray picture tube—and a few buttons. The RCA designers wanted a completely "new look," something that truly and dramatically set them apart from the competition, a product that would create a serious buzz in the market. What they came up with was wicker.

RCA produced two prototype wicker TV sets and decided that the best way to start generating some hype, or buzz, for these totally new models would be a private showing for the interior design editors of the top big-circulation house and garden magazines, like *Better Homes & Gardens* and *Good Housekeeping*. Unfortunately, the editors loved them. They enthusiastically agreed that this was a completely new look and each magazine started negotiating with RCA for the chance to break this "new product" in an upcoming issue, starting with some high-profile photography in appropriately designed room settings.

It's highly unlikely that you have seen a wicker TV set, and you probably never will. Despite the rave reviews (expressed, as it turned out, only in internal communications between the editors and RCA's normally very aggressive PR department), RCA quickly discovered that wicker TV sets are impossible to manufacture. No matter what they tried, they could not mass produce a wicker shell that fit perfectly around a TV chassis, even if they stuck to one screen size. There was always a small space somewhere along the edge of the picture tube that didn't fit just right; sometimes it was at the top of the screen, sometimes near the bottom. Or the buttons didn't fit properly in the holes. So they simply gave up.

That's the reality. It usually takes years to make things work, and longer to get them to work well enough to take them to market. And, sometimes, never.

Good Examples, Bad News

Some technologies and products are announced, get a lot of ink, and still don't come close to meeting expectations—not the vendor's and certainly not the consumer's. They were either oversold to a public that wasn't ready for them and didn't understand them, or worse, didn't need or want them in the first place. Or they're simply late to the party. More likely, they're too early. For example:

The E-Books Story: Not Exactly a Page-Turner

The Association of American Publishers, the publishing industry's principal trade organization, thinks the market for electronic book (or e-book) devices and content will grow to several billion dollars by 2004. Accenture (formerly Andersen Consulting), which is helping the AAP develop technical standards for e-books, believes there will be 26 million dedicated e-book devices in consumers' hands by the end of 2005.

If recent experience means anything, that's not likely. A survey taken in the fall of 2001 by Ipsos-NPD found that while two-thirds of online consumers in the United States were familiar with e-books, barely 3% said they were "very likely" to buy one. Scott Adams, famous for his syndicated Dilbert cartoon series, self-published an e-book, *God's Debris*, in 2001. It quickly became the best-selling e-book in the world. But he only sold about 4,500 of them, compared to the more than two million copies of his first book on paper, *The Dilbert Principle*. Adams got the message, predicting in a guest column in the *New York Times* that e-books will never exceed more than 5% of the market for pleasure reading until someone invents a way to read them without using a computer screen. "It's like taking a vacation in your cubicle," said the former engineer.

Market futurist George Forrester Colony, who heads Forrester Research, told the *New York Times*: "The technology industry is driven by thunderstorms. You see poor predictions magnified and enlarged. Asinine ideas like e-books—so much air gets pumped into them."

Book publishers continue to be hopeful, certainly wishful. Simon & Schuster has released Mary Higgins Clark's backlist of books in digital form in hopes of extending her reach. Michael Crichton's best-selling *Timeline*, published in November 1999, is available as a free e-book from BarnesandNoble.com. Walter Mosley's short stories have been published on AOL Time Warner Book's new e-book site, iPublish.com. McGraw-Hill, Houghton Mifflin, and Thomson Learning have developed e-book marketing plans. Simon & Schuster, Random House, Penguin Putnam, and HarperCollins have all signed on with Yahoo to sell their books directly to readers through the

Internet—in the event they ever want to do such a thing. Random House Children's Books has debuted its e-book publishing program, Random View Books, for Microsoft Reader, Adobe eBook Reader, and Palm Reader.

But several publishers have already backtracked. AOL Time Warner, for one, cut back its line of digital books in December 2001, citing a slump in sales. "Perhaps Mr. Gutenberg has the last laugh here," Laurence Kirschbaum, chairman of the books division, told the *New York Times*. "At some point, reality sets in and one has to be realistic about how much of an uphill climb this is going to be." (Reciprocal, the company that provided many of AOL Time Warner's technology for its digital books, went out of business only a few months earlier.)

The AAP has come around to admitting that the market is small; most of the business press and industry analysts describe it as tiny.

True, this is an entirely new market segment. And like most new consumer electronic products, dedicated e-book devices are priced high ($200 to $1,500), availability of content continues to be limited, and not every title from every publisher can be read on every device. In other words, many of these devices are technically incompatible.

Another problem is that several different types of devices are vying for attention from the few who might actually want to read a book electronically. These range from dedicated e-book devices to Palm-type PDAs and handheld and desktop PCs. There are also different file formats, content formats, digital rights management issues (who owns the rights to the e-book titles), and distribution systems.

E-books also don't take full advantage, at least not yet, of the available technology.

Brian Nadel, the editor of *Mobile Computing & Communications* magazine, has addressed this problem, pointing out that while he was impressed with the way the type of *Maestro*, Bob Woodward's look at the Federal Reserve Bank and its chairman, Alan Greenspan, mirrored that of the printed book, it would have been nice to view the printed book's 35 photos of Greenspan and five economic charts. "I would have loved to hear—not just read—Greenspan speak in his cryptic way and

then be able to link to multiple Web sites about him and the
Fed." Assuming they can get past all of these tests, how many
consumers will want to spend even an hour reading their
favorite novelist, or attempt to absorb something like *Keeping
Kosher In South Dakota* from an eye-blurring electronic display?
How long will consumers put up with recharging or buying
replacement batteries for these devices? Especially if the batteries die in the middle of a great sex scene.

The AAP standards aim to create a simulated interoperable environment for e-books for the short term that will allow
publishers to convert print books into e-books. The AAP's
suggested standards focus on numbering and metadata. The
numbering standard is based on an existing technique called
a Digital Object Identifier, which is used by the scientific,
medical, and technical communities for online content. The
metadata standard indicates how data books should be represented and includes information about the author, content,
and business rules—like the information provided in a card
catalog entry.

Book publishers are trying to avoid having to compete with
dot-coms and authors themselves who could sell digital files of
their most successful titles, just as they are trying to crank up e-
book sales. Horror story writer Stephen King skipped around
his traditional publishers to sell a new serial novel directly to
his readers in a digital format over the Internet. King offered his
book, *The Plant*, a chapter at a time with an easy payment plan,
but readers's attention span faded quickly. Worse, less than half
of King's subscribers paid for many of the chapters they downloaded (horrors!). Another problem for King was that, because
of his huge success as novelist, he was able to garner lots of free
publicity nationally about his online miseries. But he was not
equipped to generate the publicity and handle the distribution
usually provided to authors by traditional book publishers.

John Romanos, president of Simon & Schuster, told the
New York Times toward the end of 2000, "The logic of electronic books is pretty hard to refute. We see it as an incremen-
tal increase in sales as a new form of books for adults and
especially for the next generation of readers." A year later,

Simon & Schuster announced that even though the sale of these books was very skimpy, it would open its own online store to sell digital editions of its books directly to consumers. The reason for this change in thinking, the publisher said, was in response to requests from visitors to its Web site to be able to buy books directly. Now, Simon & Schuster said these people can pay for and download electronic files for reading on their computer screens.

Part of book publishers' thinking is that today's high-tech teens will become the early adopters for e-books. At least that's what Scholastic Inc., is hoping. Barbara Marcus, Scholastic's president, told the Jupiter Media Forum in early 2001 that she sees teens as a natural fit for e-books, as long as they're affordable, lightweight, and easy to use.

Whatever happens, the authors (Stephen King notwithstanding) and their agents are making sure they're also covered. In July 2001, in a decision that could put authors and their agents in the position of reselling the digital rights to a previously published work, a federal judge in New York ruled that the term "book" in book contracts with authors does not necessarily include electronic books. Random House, which tried to block Internet startup RosettaBooks from selling digital files with the contents of eight Random House novels, said at the time that it planned to appeal. Random House's view is that an e-book is a book which, it says, means it's theirs. More recently, Random House has backtracked on e-books, essentially killing its AtRandom imprint in recognition of the scant demand. Are there enough e-readers in the world to make this technology a marketing success? The Electronic Book Newsstand Association (EBNA) was formed in January 2001 to boost the awareness of e-reader devices among publishers and consumers. EBNA wants to distribute news, periodicals, and other information via portable reader devices. It says that studies show that American consumers spend far more time reading newspapers and magazines than books. Matthew Benner, director of BarnesandNoble.com's digital book group, told the *New York Times*, "We expect these devices to become the dominant platform for periodical publishing throughout the 21st Century."

In fairness, few people have experienced e-books, but the EBNA's argument seems weak. Checking new headlines, stock market quotes and sports scores from a portable electronic device, yes. News stories and features? Not likely.

If e-books are ever going to have a shot at success, it may be for special applications, such as custom-printed children's books on very cheap (and hopefully rugged) digital devices. Another new wrinkle: publishers are adding author interviews to their e-books and are beginning to offer some bilingual models so readers can switch between, say, English and Spanish. Or technical reference material. Another possibility is local libraries, more of which are making e-books available. Indeed, library associations have been lobbying for the development of inexpensive electronic readers for library use. One drawback, at least, for the moment, is that you have to take what the libraries have loaded into the readers.

The WAP Flap

One of the most widely covered issues in the wireless communications industry in 1997 was how to get wireless handsets to tap into the Internet. Several companies, including the three market-share leaders, Nokia, Ericsson, and Motorola, were pretty sure they had the answer in something called the Wireless Application Protocol, or WAP, which these companies helped develop as a nonproprietary, global technical specification. WAP would enable wireless service subscribers to access Web-based information from mobile or portable cellphones or PDAs.

It sounded pretty good at the time. WAP meant the wireless Internet was here. We could now access the Internet from just about anywhere and at anytime. You couldn't open a business publication or even many daily newspapers without readying something about this wonderful new development that would make our lives so much more productive. Using a WAP-enabled wireless device, you could check the traffic en route to the airport. If traffic is going to hold you up, you could check the train schedule and then purchase a train ticket online instead of driving. On the way to the airport, you could select your seat, check in for the flight, and reserve a special meal.

You could also use WAP for message notification and call management, e-mail, mapping and locator services, weather alerts, news, sports, e-commerce transactions, and banking services.

Cellular phone and other equipment manufacturers were drawn to WAP because it had the potential to generate the critical mass needed for them to open up new product and service opportunities in wireless communications—actually generate new revenue by getting people to spend more time on their cellphones. Network operators supported WAP because it seemed to have minimal risk and investment, and they thought it would help operators decrease churn (keep people from switching wireless carriers, usually for a cheaper plan or more free "airtime" hours), cut costs, and increase revenues by improving existing value-added services and adding new services.

It looked like it couldn't miss, especially with so many of the top telecom companies teaming up to develop and promote the technology. So, why did so many industry analysts and users start referring to WAP as "What *A* Pain?" And why have there been so many articles like the one in *Wireless Week* that started with sentence, "Is the Wireless Application Protocol dead?" under a headline, "Warning to WAP: Reinvent Or Waste Away."

David Haskins, the managing editor of the online AllNet-Devices news service, wrote in July 2000: "Will consumers embrace WAP or is it just another example of over-hyped BWC (Because We Can) technology that the public will ignore?"

Another industry magazine, *America's Network*, was equally uncharitable after conducting a "WAP Test Drive." It wrote, "Using a WAP service is like using the Internet in 1995. You know it's a great idea and you really want to try it out. But when you actually test it, you find that you don't really want to do it again."

Phone.com, a leading proponent and early WAP pioneer, claimed that 100,000 software developers had registered for its WAP developer program and more than 500 companies were actively participating in the WAP Forum, formed in 1998, presumably spending millions collectively to bring WAP-based products to market. But few people were actually using WAP. And those who were, weren't exactly thrilled by it.

In its defense, some analysts and industry supporters suggested that WAP offered a different paradigm for accessing the Web from a PC in the office or at home. That's true, but it got more complicated, with highly publicized complaints that data retrieval was slow, that applications and services were lacking, that WAP was often difficult to navigate, and that cellphone and PDA screens are simply too small for any reasonable text-driven application. The Nielsen Norman Group said after conducting a survey in London, that WAP usability is "failing miserably." Nielson Norman said, "Companies shouldn't waste money fielding WAP services that nobody will use while WAP usability remains so poor. Instead, they should sit out the current generation of WAP while planning their mobile Internet strategy." The WAP Forum, the technologies' support group, quickly pointed out that the study was based on only 20 users and "lacks the basis on which to draw any meaningful conclusions." It didn't help that another market study published by Forrester Research in mid-2000 pointed out that 72% of U.S. households have no interest in receiving data on their wireless phones and 75% are uncomfortable with wireless e-commerce. (As of the end of 2000, the WAP Forum estimated there were more than 40 million WAP-enabled devices in circulation. The organization could not say at the time how many of these handsets subscribers are actually using WAP, but they guessed that it was in the four to five million range.)

WAP took another public flogging in Europe when articles began to appear that anyone using a GSM phone (Global System for Mobile Communications is the digital cellular standard used throughout Europe and part of the United States) didn't actually need WAP. They could get similar results with SMS (Short Messaging Service), which is popular in Europe for delivering text to pagers.

The Meta Group, another market research organization, put WAP's principal developer, Openwave Systems, on the defensive when it reported that as many as 90% of corporate users that purchased WAP-enabled phones have abandonded the data capabilities of these phones. According to Meta, limited content, slow networks, and generally poor user ergonomics have not met the high user expectations and hype that accompanied WAP-enabled devices when they were first introduced.

WAP also faced competition in Japan from i-mode, a hugely popular wireless Internet-level system, developed by the country's largest mobile carrier, NTT DoCoMo. Introduced in the spring of 1999, i-mode at one point was adding more than 40,000 new subscribers a day in Japan and claimed 17 million users by the end of 2000. To call i-mode a cash cow for NTT DoCoMo is a disservice to the company: Just one of its many unbundled features, sending a cartoon to subscribers every day for a monthly fee of about $1, generates more than $120 million annually for NTT.

Like WAP, i-mode enables users to access e-mail and Internet services with wireless phones and computers. Unlike WAP, i-mode is based on packet data technology, which means that it is always online; you do not have to dial up every time you want access to the Internet or e-mail. Using packet technology also means that i-mode users are charged only for the information they receive, not for how long they stay online. (I-mode also represents a cultural breakthrough. It was bound to be a success, analysts like to point out, because in contrast to the United States, where PC market penetration is huge, the wireless Web is pretty much the only experience the Japanese have with the Internet.) The difficulties with WAP and the success of i-mode have led to growing interest in i-mode outside Japan, mainly in Europe. NTT DoCoMo could also expand the use of i-mode through joint ventures with U.S. wireless operators— AT&T Wireless has licensed i-mode, giving it a potentially strong jump-start in the United States—a particularly interesting prospect if WAP doesn't begin to gain wider acceptance in the United States. Some wireless carriers have talked about supporting both WAP and i-mode. Yet another possibility kicked around the industry is that WAP will be replaced by the Java programming language from Sun Microsystems, which abstracts data on bytecodes so that the same code runs on any operating system. In fact, i-mode will eventually allow users to tap into Java technology, providing even more services to i-mode subscribers.

Another issue lurking in the background, and one that doesn't instill a lot of confidence in wireless manufacturers who are asked to invest in these things, is, who owns the technology? While WAP has been originally promoted as an "open" protocol, Geoworks, a specialist in wireless data communications services and technologies, told the WAP Forum and its members in May 1999 that its patented technology is "employed as essential technology" in the WAP standard and that it planned to license this technology. Phone.com challenged Geoworks' patents as invalid. However, Ericsson, Matsushita Electric (the parent company of Panasonic), Toshiba, and others have lent some credibility to Geoworks' patent claim when they signed a cross-licensing arrangement giving them the right to use Geoworks' WAP technology.

This is also about content. Analysts believe that as the number of practical applications available to WAP users grows, WAP will begin to gain a following. WAP may also find broad acceptance as a sales representatives' automation tool with WAP-enabled phones for checking customer information, checking inventories, and tracking order status while on the road.

Can more than 500 companies be wrong? The jury (in this case, the market) is still out, but the same question is being asked about Bluetooth.

Is WAP an interim technology? Even many of the most objective industry observers don't believe so. WAP will continue to add popular features such as TCP/IP, multimedia, and color graphics, but WAP device owners will still have to contend with tiny keyboards and displays—at least until voice recognition technology and virtual displays, which magnify 2-inch screens into what appear to be 17-inch displays, make huge leaps into portable communications products.

Biting into Bluetooth

The business and technical press coverage of Bluetooth has been constant and often brutal. And for the most part, rightfully so. "Are we getting ahead of ourselves—again?" wrote a technology magazine editor in his monthly column. "It's got momentum, it's got mass, and it's got great PR." Then there were headlines like, "Bluetooth Riddled With Cavities" and "Bluetooth Still Teething." A more to the point headline would have been, "Bluetooth Vendors Bite Off More Than They Can Chew."

Bluetooth was designed to enable spontaneous connectivity between cellular phones, mobile computers, personal digital assistants (PDAs), and other wireless devices.

Initially conceived as a wireless replacement for cable hookups for portable consumer electronic products, Bluetooth has become a digital transmission standard for short-range links between laptop computers, cellular phones, PDAs, and other electronic devices. But there is an important difference from other wireless networks: It offers what the Bluetooth community calls "unconscious" or "hidden" computing. Bluetooth-enabled products will be designed to automatically seek each other out and configure themselves into piconetworks, which can, among other things, forward e-mail received on a cellular phone in a person's pocket to the notebook computer or laptop in a nearby briefcase. Bluetooth can also exchange business cards with someone passed on the street or in a bar or restaurant if given permission to do so, "opening up whole new blind dating opportunities," according to a Merrill Lynch research report. It can download data from a digital camera to a PC or cellphone. Children sitting in the front of a school bus could play games with children sitting in the back of the same bus. In fixed applications, it can replace hardwired connections with wireless Internet access points in airports, hotel lobbies, and conference centers. A Finnish telecom operator has even demonstrated a Bluetooth-enabled vending machine, allowing consumers to buy products out of the machine by transmitting an account code from a Bluetooth phone or PDA.

Why "Bluetooth?" Because someone at Ericsson suggested naming this new development after King Harald of Denmark, nicknamed Bluetooth, who is credited with uniting the warring factions of Denmark and Norway in the 10th century, when he reigned. Ericsson figured it could do the same with its Bluetooth—unite wireless devices everywhere.

Bluetooth is supposed to be the "next big thing." But it has had some problems getting out of the chute, most of them technical. Ericsson began exploring short-range, low-power, low-cost wireless technologies in 1994. By 1998, Ericsson was convinced it had something important and that it was far enough along in its development to move forward, but it needed help to develop the technology into an open, global standard and to promote the concept. To pull this off, Ericsson teamed with four other heavyweights—IBM, Toshiba, Intel, and Nokia. Together, they formed what became known as the Bluetooth Special Interest Group (SIG), which eventually grew to more than 2,000 company members worldwide.

The hype has been huge, as have been the expectations. Market research organizations projected that more than a billion Bluetooth-enabled devices would be on the market by 2004. One of them, the Gartner Group, said it expected Bluetooth to become a "defining force" in portable electronic products. Merrill Lynch estimated that by 2005, Bluetooth would be in 95% of the world's cellular phones (that's more than a billion phones), 95% of wireless headsets (700 million), 90% of PCs (400 million), 50% of all of the printers sold that year (109 million), and 60% of digital cameras (64 million).

But there were problems. Virtually none of the earliest Bluetooth products tested worked as designed—they simply would not communicate. Testing was difficult because there were no instruments to measure many of Bluetooth's unique functions. It didn't help that the target price for Bluetooth integrated circuits (ICs), set somewhere in the early going at $5—a bit high for a consumer electronics device—didn't seem attainable on any scale until at least 2002, possibly later.

Bluetooth security was another issue, but it stayed in the background until two researchers at Lucent Technologies announced they had found flaws in the technology that could permit anyone to eavesdrop on a digital conversation or even to determine a user's identity. Although the Lucent researchers said the problem could be fixed fairly easily, the disclosure generated more negative press for Bluetooth, focusing mostly on the technology's use in high-traffic areas, such as airports and conference centers.

Another serious issue was interference. Millions of products already in use operate in the same frequency range as Bluetooth—2.4 gigahertz (GHz)—such as microwave ovens, garage door openers, audio remote control devices, toys, the newest cordless phone models, as well as two competing technologies—wireless local area networks, which link offices and factories in buildings or campus-type settings, and HomeRF, which is the standard for wireless home and small office networks capable of linking multiple PCs for other wireless devices. Moving Bluetooth to a higher frequency has been discussed in Bluetooth and regulatory circles, but that could be years off.

Then there's the brand. Bluetooth SIG leaders were deathly afraid that some companies, particularly small startups and no-name Asian toy and accessories makers, would jump the gun with Bluetooth-labeled products before they are technically ready to interoperate with fully "certified" Bluetooth devices and give the brand a bad name. Simon Ellis, communications marketing manager for the mobile and handheld product group at Intel and marketing chairman of the SIG, told *Wireless Systems Design* magazine in December 1998: "It's terribly important that [Bluetooth] not be overhyped, setting up the possibility for disappointment in the marketplace when the actual products start appearing."

Bluetooth also has competition. The most serious is the IEEE 802.11 technical standard for wireless local area networks. Initially developed for use in offices and factories, a number of versions of this technology are emerging that could give Bluetooth a serious run for its money, particularly in fixed wireless applications. Another would-be competitor is infrared (IR) technology, which consumers have been using for years to change their TV channels and adjust the volume on their stereo systems. IR is also a feature that is built into virtually every notebook computer, mainly to wirelessly exchange business cards and to dump text material into an IR-equipped printer at very short range.

The installed base of IR-equipped products easily tops 250 million globally. But unlike Bluetooth, which is a radio and is only range-limited, IR must operate line-of-sight (the IR ports of different products must be aimed at each other) and operates within a narrow angle (a 30-degree maximum cone) and at very short range. It also transmits data at relatively slow speeds, which helps explain why few people actually use the IR feature in their portable devices. (Toshiba estimated a few years ago that barely 5% of its notebook computer customers used the IR function.) IrDA, the Infrared Data Association, claims this has changed with the growing population of PDA users and says usage is now up to at least 40% among Palm users. IrDA calls them "loyal Palm beamers." IrDA also believes IR use is a cultural issue because it is very popular in Japan and Europe, particularly for exchanging business cards and short text messages. (In fact, Casio's IR-enabled QV2000 digital camera is available virtually everywhere but the United States.)

Bottom line, the delivery of Bluetooth products on any kind of a meaningful scale was more than a year behind schedule. Almost everyone anticipated a significant number and variety of Bluetooth products on retailers shelves by the end of 2000. The reality check came when a worldwide survey of design engineers indicated that most of them didn't expect their companies to *begin* delivering Bluetooth-enabled devices in any significant numbers until at least 2003—not a pretty picture for a technology that is only effective and useful when it reaches a critical mass; what good is a Bluetooth-enabled device if it has no one to "talk" to?

None of these problems are as serious, however, as SIG members' concerns about interoperability. As would-be Bluetooth vendors moved into 2001, few of their products had met the SIG's interoperability requirements, which means that almost none of them could actually communicate as they were supposed to.

To help speed Bluetooth products to market, the SIG waived some of the most rigorous test requirements for interoperability and allowed tests of Bluetooth products against what were called Blue Units, which were actually kits made up of key components, software, and documentation to help first-time Bluetooth design engineers accelerate the development of prototype devices. Just to complicate things, some products were ready for market before test systems had been validated and were available. Meanwhile, SIG members were developing their own test equipment for Bluetooth products and conducting "unplugfests" in which they tested their products against each other to ensure interoperability.

As reported in the November 2000 issue of *IEEE Spectrum*, "With several companies, mostly startups like San Diego's Silicon Wave and Britain's Cambridge Silicon Radio, all but betting the ranch on the success of Bluetooth, it is going to be difficult to soften the hype and face the reality of creating electronic products with an entirely new communications interface. But, then, this is supposed to be a joint effort and, as one market analyst put it, "2,000 companies can't be wrong."

Calling Big LEO

Blame Arthur C. Clarke. In 1945, long before he created the highly successful *Space Odyssey* films (2001 and 2010) with Stanley Kubrick, Clarke came up with the idea of a global network of communications satellites, circling the earth in geostationary orbit. Using this concept and the technology, anyone would be able to talk to and eventually send data, faxes, and video to anyone just about anywhere in the world. Since then, thousands of these satellites have been launched into orbit, and satellite communications has become a multibillion dollar industry.

But most of these satellites serve fixed terminals (the phone on your desk, for example), and handle mainly international traffic and phones in rural or remote areas, such as oil rigs miles out in the ocean. Eventually, commercial aircraft and ships began to use mobile satcom services. More recently, satellite networks have been developed that enable people to use a portable phone, not much bigger than most cellular phones, to call anyone in the world at any time simply by dialing their satellite phone number.

A significant technical achievement, but who needs this? Initially, the developers of this technology thought it would be an immediate and huge success in underdeveloped and developing countries, most of which are saddled with antiquated telecommunications infrastructures. Satellite-based kiosks would be set up in even the most rural locations so that anyone could call long-lost colleagues and family members anywhere in the world. Also, government agencies, businesses, and even VIPs who must always be in touch could take advantage of this new communications opportunity. In time, as the price of the phones and the rates came down, the service would trickle down to small- and mid-level business travelers and small business owners.

One possible scenario: You're sitting in your office in Bridgewater, New Jersey, and your partner is in Malaysia, on her way to make a sales presentation to a potential new client. You just came up with some new numbers that will vastly enhance your chances of getting the account. You have no idea where she is at the moment but, judging by the time, she's probably somewhere in downtown Kuala Lumpur, en route to her meeting. Fortunately, you can reach her by simply direct-dialing her portable satcom phone, just as you would make any other phone call.

It sounded pretty good during the nearly 15 years that Motorola and others promoted this technology and dumped literally billions of dollars into developing it. But the hype, which included literally hundreds of articles in business and telecom industry magazines (some of them produced by Motorola's own engineers and marketing staff), countless presentations at conferences and seminars, and a very slick in-house-developed quarterly magazine with a "we are the world" flavored text, got way ahead of the reality, which led to some very costly failures.

What can you say about a company that began commercial operations on November 1, 1998, filed for Chapter 11 bankruptcy protection on August 13, 1999, and officially terminated its service on March 17, 2000? The company, known as Iridium and created and supported largely by Motorola, projected in 1997 that it would have 650,000 voice subscribers and 350,000 paging subscribers worldwide by 2000. That should be enough, it said, to meet its market goals. In fact, with a total of fewer than 55,000 subscribers at that point, Motorola was ready to allow its satellites to "deorbit"; that is, literally fall into the ocean rather than continue supporting them.

Iridium wasn't alone. In 1994, Craig McCaw, who had just sold his company, McCaw Cellular, to AT&T for $12 billion, and Microsoft's Bill Gates pooled some of their fortunes and formed Teledesic LLC to develop a high-speed network of 840 communications satellites. With great fanfare, McCaw and Gates said the new space-based network would be in operation beginning in 1998. Those plans were still on hold in 2001 while McCaw tended to his other mobile satcom property, ICO Global Communications Ltd., which filed for bankruptcy only a few weeks after Iridium sought the same protection.

Another mobile satcom hopeful, Globalstar Telecommunications Ltd., a consortium led by Loral Space and Communications and Qualcomm (other partners include China Telecom, DaimlerChrysler Aerospace, and Vodafone Group plc), announced plans to launch a 48-satellite system with operations beginning by 1997. That start date slipped a few years and with only 44,000 subscribers (analysts believe that Globalstar needs 1.6 million customers just to cover its costs and service its debt), Globalstar told the Securities & Exchange Commission in April 2001 that it "may be forced to seek protection under the federal bankruptcy laws" if it couldn't restructure its debt. In February 2002, with only 66,000 subscribers, Globalstar filed for Chapter 11 protection but said a new company will be created whose assets will be held by the company's bondholders and unsecured debt holders.

Part of the problem for Iridium seems to be that its leadership got a little too excited by the rapid growth of cellular and the Internet and thought this would quickly translate into an instant opportunity for totally portable, if somewhat pricey, direct-dial global communications. But how many people who have been using a cellular phone (which may have been free, along with hundreds or thousands of free airtime hours) really need another phone that's nearly twice the size of a cellphone and that costs $3,500 to purchase and $3 to $9 a minute per call—even if it does receive direct-dial calls just about anywhere in the world? Another problem either glossed over by Motorola or discounted as not a big issue was that Iridium's radio signals and those of the other mobile satellite services were not powerful enough to reach inside most buildings where people work and live and spend a lot of time. They have enough problems reaching the streets between tall city buildings. McCaw figured this out fairly early and has been trying to overcome these problems by getting Federal Communications Commission approval to install enough radio towers in key locations so that ICO would resemble a cellular system in urban areas, with its signals reaching everywhere.

How did all of this get started in the first place?

Iridium was first conceived by Motorola as a network of 77 satellites (hence, Iridium, the element whose atom has 77 orbiting electrons) orbiting 420 miles above the earth, transmitting voice and data satellite-to-satellite until they reached the nearest ground station. At this point, they would be connected to the public telephone network and switched to the caller or callee, just like any other phone call or data connection. However, even before the first satellite was launched, engineers figured out a way to reduce the number of satellites needed for the system to 66. (Motorola had already invested so much in the system and the name that it decided to stick with Iridium.) In generic industry terms, the Iridium satellite system was usually referred to as a Big LEO because it offered both voice and data and operated in *low-earth orbit*. Little LEOs, which were to come later, provided data-only services.

Things started to get a little complicated when two long-established communication satellite service providers, the International Maritime Satellite Service, or Inmarsat, which provides global communications to the shipping industry, and the International Telecommunications Satellite Organization, now known simply as Intelsat, a consortium of 139-country signatories providing voice, data, and video communication services, decided they wanted a piece of the global mobile satcom action.

As international treaty organizations, Intelsat and Inmarsat had important advantages over the new mobile satellite services. One of these was easier access to orbital slots in space as well as to the most efficient spectrum assignments. Another was tax privileges and antitrust immunities that the private companies would never have. Any private concern that wanted to compete with Intelsat and Inmarsat was also required, under the treaty agreements, to coordinate its business plans with the treaty-protected organizations to ensure that they did not significantly harm or cause technical interference to Intelsat and Inmarsat. It didn't take long for the U.S. General Accounting Office (GAO) to publish a study questioning the fairness of Intelsat's entry into the mobile communication satellite arena, which the GAO said, "may be impeding the flourishing of a private market and the benefits it can bring to consumers."

McCaw managed to save ICO in May 2000 with an infusion of $1.2 billion and a new plan to reintroduce the service as a smaller, slightly less ambitious version of Teledesic. Like Iridium, ICO said that it intended to go after niche markets like shipping and long-haul trucking. Rescheduled for launch in 2003, New ICO—an interim name used by McCaw—planned to use a special device that attaches to existing portable handsets rather than developing new, costly, and dedicated phones for its service. The tab for getting this venture off the ground was an estimated $2.5 billion on top of what had already been invested in the venture. More recently, however, with McCaw at the controls, Teledesic said it would reduce the size of its global satcom network to just 30 satellites and signed a contract with Alenia Spazio, an Italian firm, to produce Teledesic's first two satellites. The contract represents the bare minimum required for Teledesic to hang on to its spectrum assigned to it by the FCC. Teledesic now plans to be in operation in 2005, but it must obtain new regulatory approvals for its new orbital satellite scheme, which will focus on delivering high-speed data services. McCaw had considered merging ICO and Teledesic into a single company, probably called ICO-Teledesic, and marketing its services jointly. That's no longer likely, because McCaw says he wants to keep ICO and Teledesic independent as the needs of satellite services evolve globally.

Iridium, meanwhile, has regrouped, also under a new name. The bankruptcy sale has been approved, and a new CEO who, with other investors, has acquired its assets for $25 million, has taken over what is now Iridium Satellite LLC. The new Iridium team has thrown out the old marketing plan in favor of attacking niche markets, such as maritime, petroleum, construction, forestry, and emergency services. It also signed the U.S. Defense Information Systems Agency to a $72 million service contract.

Will these systems now fly commercially? Going after vertical businesses and the military should work if the Big LEOs can hold down their operating costs. Under the new marketing plan, subscribers get a second-generation Motorola handset, which is much cheaper and closer in size to a cellular phone than the original model, and will pay about 80 cents a minute for phone service. The easy answer is that time will tell, but the niche and high-speed Internet approaches the Big LEOs plan to pursue may be their last chance to succeed.

HDTV—Not a Pretty Picture

Does anyone even remember what HDTV stands for? It's high-definition television. And we have been hearing and reading about it for almost 20 years.

The earliest piece of HDTV hype came from, of all places, a widely reported 1987 Federal Communications Commission advisory committee study that described HDTV as "an economic opportunity of almost unparalleled proportions." Anyone who had actually seen HDTV at the time probably would have agreed. Even then, the picture was startlingly clear, as good as any large-print color photo. Press reports were glowing, referring to "quality that dazzles."

But HDTV has faced one technological and political hurdle after another, mainly from broadcasters (both local stations and the networks) and local and cable TV operators who don't want to spend the money to upgrade their systems. It has also been hard to convince consumers that they really need a TV set with improved picture quality that's going to cost several thousand dollars.

HDTV took one of its first widely publicized hits in 1996 in *The Unpredictable Certainty—Information Infrastructure Through 2000*, published by the Computer Science and Telecommunications Board of the National Science Foundation's National Research Council. In a chapter titled "Making Technologies Work," members of the National Information Infrastructure 2000 Steering Committee—made up mostly of research executives of leading technology companies and university professors—said they "generally discounted the impact of HDTV as a force shaping communications and information-related behavior and markets for the next 5 to 7 years, given HDTV's high initial prices and very limited sales." The authors also expressed the belief that "it will be even longer before a significant amount of HDTV-compatible programming will be available." The committee considered the availability of new spectrum for other uses to be more important than a higher-fidelity television viewing experience. "TV programming displays on PCs are growing," the committee wrote, "presenting prospects for enhancing and otherwise using those images."

The industry sold 625,000 HDTV-ready receivers to dealers in 2000, a fivefold increase over 1999. But when you add it all up, less than 3% of all TV sales in the United States reported by the Consumer Electronics Association are digital. And those numbers represent sales to dealers, not consumers. The real number is closer to 425,000.

It has been a tough pitch. In 1993, after more than 10 years of well-financed research and development by several organizations in the United States, Japan, and Europe, a "Grand Alliance" was formed by three groups that were competing to develop a technical standard for an American HDTV system. (Japan got a big jump on the rest of the world with its HDTV system, but it's analog based, and it is not selling as hoped.) Taking a "best of the best" approach, Grand Alliance members selected what they thought were the strongest elements of each of their systems and came to an agreement on an advanced TV standard.

In 1995, the FCC's Advanced Television Standard Committee (ATSC) endorsed the alliance's proposal for 18 different standards from which broadcasters could chose. Broadcasters would then have to acquire the equipment needed to transmit in an HDTV format. Special programming would have to be developed and produced. TV manufacturers would then have to build the sets with circuitry capable of handling all of the different formats.

In 1997, the FCC set aside the spectrum needed for digital broadcasting. It established a nine-year transition period for U.S. consumers to completely switch over from their current analog sets to digital television (DTV) or to add digital-to-analog converters to their old sets. During this time, broadcasters were to begin transmitting digital as well as their usual analog TV signals, using a second channel allocated for DTV. In 2006, according to FCC rules, or until digital broadcasts reach 85% of U.S. households, whichever comes later, analog broadcasts will cease and broadcasters will give up their old analog frequencies to the FCC to be used for other services. (Note: It took more than 20 years for color TV and 16 years for VCRs to reach that level of market penetration. Color TV was introduced in the mid-1950s and didn't start to outsell black-and-white TV sets until the mid-1970s. And color probably wouldn't have grown that fast if David Sarnoff, who ran RCA at the time, had not personally ordered NBC, then owned by RCA, to broadcast all of its prime time programs in color.)

It is unlikely that the FCC deadline will be met because broadcasters are dragging their feet and Congress is unlikely to force the issue. Broadcasters donated millions of dollars to members of Congress between 1987 and 1996 and lobbied the Telecommunications Act of 1996 heavily enough to win free licenses for new spectra valued by industry analysts at $70 billion.

Gary Chapman, president and CEO of LIN Television Corp. and chairman of the board of the National Association of Broadcasters, put his best spin on his industry before the House Telecommunications Subcommittee when he said that broadcasters are developing and implementing various DTV services "in keeping with the flexibility Congress complemented in the '96 Act." In fact, most broadcasters are in no hurry to offer HDTV. At the end of 2000, only 173 out of a total of 1,288 TV stations were broadcasting in a digital format in the United States. When they finally upgrade, many of them will use their new digital channels for an entirely new revenue stream—providing commercial data services in competition with others who currently do the same thing. What some broadcasters called "left-over bandwidth" until they figured out they could make more money with it (they now call it "enhanced television") will enable them to transmit commercial data over the air, including Web content, stock reports, and printable electronic coupons. In more technical terms, each 6 megahertz DTV channel can transport data at 19.39 megabits per second, which is 346 times faster than a 56K modem. This can be used for television, non-TV data, or a combination of both.

Television set manufacturers have more than held up their end. They have introduced about 200 different digital TV-related products, including DTV and HDTV monitors, integrated sets, and stand-alone set-top boxes. With broadcasts moving slowly and little programming available, TV manufacturers now appear to be in no hurry to produce HDTV, or HDTV-ready, models. Gary Shapiro, president of the Consumer Electronics Association, asked his members in *Vision*, the association's magazine, to "keep the pressure on local broadcasters, and reward those—maybe even with your HDTV ads—that are helping, rather than hurting, our momentum."

They're not having much luck. Most DTV manufacturers' sales have been DTV and HDTV displays that require the addition of a set-top box to receive digital broadcasts. In 1999, 17% of the total DTV products sold (including monitors, integrated sets, and digital set-top receivers) were capable of receiving digital broadcasts. This trend will likely continue if some broadcasters continue to challenge the DTV broadcast standard or insist on using DTV primarily as a subscription service.

With prices ranging from $2,500 to $6,000, most industry analysts believe that it is unlikely that one million HDTV sets will be shipped before 2003. A point of reference: About 130 million color TV sets are manufactured in the world every year. It comes down to the chicken-and-egg thing. Broadcasters say they don't want to build-out their digital system until programmers develop more material in a digital format, and TV manufacturers don't want to crank up their digital set production until more TV stations begin broadcasting digital signals. Consumer confusion about the terminology (DTV, HDTV, standard definition television, and SDTV) doesn't help.

If the programming transition continues at its current pace, the Consumer Electronics Association expects DTV penetration to slow. To meet its moderate projection of 30% market penetration by 2006, broadcasters will have to step-up the pace and provide more substantial HDTV programming. With an accelerated commitment from broadcasters, the CEA believes that it can reach or exceed 50% penetration by 2006.

In February 2002, the National Association of Broadcasters and Consumer Electronics Association began a campaign to promote HDTV, using a series of specially developed commercials and "watch parties" in three cities—Houston, Indianapolis, and Portland, Oregon—with network-affiliated TV stations already broadcasting digital TV signals.

The question for consumers now is, how much better is HDTV reception than their current TV reception? Is it more than $2,000 better? If not, when will broadcasters, programmers, TV manufacturers, and regulators get it together and make HDTV a true mass market reality? How long will it take for the price of these sets to drop to a much more comfortable $500?

Stay tuned.

Information Appliances (Or Home on the Digital Range)

How many times have you read about or seen a feature or a news clip on TV on the "kitchen of the future"? How often have you been told that you can start your morning coffee from your bedroom as soon as you sit up in bed, or turn on your lights and TV simply by dialing a code into your cellular phone from thousands of miles away? Or link your refrigerator to the Internet?

The goal of a growing number of companies is to create an entirely new market segment by developing a standardized platform that would enable your stove to communicate with Internet-enabled information appliances. These IAs, as they're called, are variously described as a stripped-down, low-cost, easy-to-use, sometimes special-purpose alternative to the personal computer that is usually tied into the Internet. "There will come a time, in the not-too-distant future," says the Consumer Electronics Association, "when this will all seem ordinary, even passé."

Maybe.

Hype-generated as it is, this market has stalled before it got into second gear. What some still call the home integrated systems (HIS) market has grown very gradually since a device called X-10 first introduced automated lighting control in the late 1970s. More than 100 million X-10 devices were sold through 1999, but even the Consumer Electronics Association admits that the X-10 is an anomaly in the 20-year history of home control.

According to a 1998 survey by the association called Integrated Home Systems Potential, only 12% of consumers have some type of HIS, which the association defines as a system that allows consumers to manage some or all of their home's lighting, audio and video, security, energy, and communications.

The hype has been rampant for years. Manufacturers of small appliances (electric products that usually sit on top of a counter) and major appliances (such as dishwashers, ovens, and washing machines), along with some consumer electronic manufacturers continue to talk a good game, but they know that a mass market for automating this stuff is a long way off. "The biggest problem," wrote one magazine editor, "is the apathy of the end user to such systems." In other words, very few people actually want it or perceive a need for a refrigerator that tells them or their PC when they're almost out of milk. In fact, of those households that do not have a home system, 46% of those surveyed by the Consumer Electronics Association said they did not have a need for an integrated home network.

The technology is in place, even if the market is still very much in limbo. Current technical "solutions" include Microsoft's Universal Plug-and-Play (UPnP) and Jini, which is being heavily promoted by Sun Microsystems. Both systems can intercommunicate, and both have received strong backing from major appliance manufacturers, but consumers still aren't on board. GE, Maytag, and Whirlpool each plan to develop refrigerators and ovens that can be connected to both the Internet and/or a home network. Why are they doing this?

"It's fairly easy to imagine the benefit, given that many savvy cooks already log on in the kitchen to download recipes," says the Consumer Electronics Association, albeit from their home PC. As the trade association sees it, an Internet-enabled stove would be able to set itself according to cooking instructions downloaded to it from a Frugal Gourmet Web site. At the same time, the Internet fridge could take any inventory of the ingredients needed for the recipe. The fridge could also print out a grocery list and place the order with an online grocer. A bar code reader built onto the face of the microwave could automatically set the power level and timer the instant the cook waved a package of food in front of it. A residential gateway could leverage other Web-based services such as performance upgrades, warranty registration, remote diagnostics, and energy management features.

The next obvious step is to have these "connected" appliances communicate with each other over a universal home network. Whirlpool's concept refrigerator, which could be on the market in a few years, features a built-in touchscreen used to access the Internet, store messages, and control other electronic devices in the home. You can detach the touchscreen to cue the stereo, adjust the intensity of the lights, and post a family schedule. Similar products are in development by other manufacturers.

The Massachusetts Institute of Technology (MIT) has been playing around with kitchen technology for years. To pursue a "vision of the future" in domestic technology, interested graduate students and faculty advisors have formed a group cleverly named Counter Intelligence, which is supported by a tightly knit set of projects called Kitchen Sync. With Kitchen Sync, a microwave oven could, for example, correlate cooking time to weight. Another Kitchen Sync development is Mr. Java, an intelligent coffee machine, which can identify the user of the cup and prepare coffee to the cup owner's liking. Then there is the Kitchen Sync Chocolate Cake Scenario. It's right out of Star Trek. As described by grad student Joseph Kaye, you would announce "Kitchen," bringing Kitchen Sync out of its digital slumber. "I'd like to make a chocolate cake for dessert tonight." Kitchen Sync also reminds you where you put the ingredients and then offers the recipe. It also suggests ingredient substitutions, such as the use of low-fat chocolate. From there, it's only a matter of sliding the cake into the preheated oven and waiting until Kitchen Sync tells you when to take it out.

Another project keeps track of overall consumption of coffee, including dividing the data by day and by hour over time. For example, when MIT researchers first tried this a few years ago, they discovered that coffee use peaked at 11 a.m. and again at 3 p.m. This information was, according to a white paper produced by one of the graduate students at the time, of great interest to many of its sponsors, including Maxwell House and Procter & Gamble (owner of Folgers), who have spent a lot of time and effort tracking usage statistics such as these, historically by hand.

Another MIT application is a refrigerator, known as Cool I/O (for input/output), that keeps track of its contents, with the dates that an item entered the fridge or was used, and its expiration date. Also on MIT's development wish list: Cameras above stoves to ensure that a watched pot never boils over, and trash cans that tell you when they are full. Cool I/O is projected as a 10-year program in terms of actually getting it into the market.

Again, who really needs this stuff? Hardly anyone, according to Andrew M. Odlyzko, the head of the Mathematics & Cryptography Research Department at AT&T Labs, who wrote *The Visible Problems of the Invisible Computers: A Skeptical Look at Information Appliances* in 1999. Published in the online journal *First Monday* (www.firstmonday.org/issues/issue4_9/odlyzko), Odlyzko's take is that no one has really figured out how to make these information appliances work together. "The interaction of the coffee pot, the car, the smart fridge, and the networked camera will create a new layer of complexity. In the rush toward the digital era, we will continue to live right on the edge of intolerable frustration."

This hasn't stopped the market research community from priming the IA pump. In 2000, Parks Associates projected that information appliances will outstrip PCs in the United States by as early as 2001. Parks said its research suggests that 22 million in-home information appliances (excluding Internet-enabled mobile phones and telematics systems in vehicles) will ship in the United States in 2001, compared with 18 million PCs in the same year. By 2005, Parks forecasted, total revenue from all information appliances (again, excluding Internet-enabled cellphones and telematics systems) will reach $33.7 billion. Another market researcher, International Data Corp., has been saying almost the same thing: that, by 2002, more information appliances will be sold to consumers than PCs. Dataquest also sees 2002 as IAs' watershed year, with measurable growth in TV-enabled Internet access devices, including set-top boxes and dedicated Web tablets.

And while PCs are pretty much compatible with each other, most new and emerging information appliances are not. By one analyst's count, at least 60 different companies were racing to get an information appliance to market before the end of 2000. So far, few have made any formal product introductions, and one of the biggest reasons is that they can't figure out what system architecture will work best in a market where manufacturers are pretty much doing their own thing. For the moment, there are no technical standards for IA. And fixing this problem is not one of the stated goals of the Internet Home Alliance.

Formed in October 2000 this nonprofit association of high-tech manufacturers and retailers has chosen to focus on "catalyzing the home technology industry and fueling mass adoption of connected technology by focusing on solving consumer dilemmas through the Internet Lifestyle." It will have its hands full. 3Com, an early IA player and hardly a lightweight in the consumer marketplace, shut down its Web appliance division early in 2001 and discontinued its retail product, the Audrey Web tablet. At about the same time, Gateway, which barely got its IA product out of the box, said it was "rethinking" its next move in the category.

Why did 3Com drop Audrey? "While we continue to believe in the potential for Audrey," 3Com said in a news release, "there are indications the market will take longer to develop than originally planned and require additional investment." Which 3Com indicated it was not prepared to do at the time.

Netpliances introduced i-opener, powered by AT&T World-Net Service and scheduled to be available from QVC, the electronic retailer, but that also hasn't gone very far. Vtech, meanwhile, introduced its e-Mail PostBox and Address Book to Yahoo! customers in the fall of 2000, but the company has since revised its business plan, merging its IA and PDA units into its consumer telephone business division. Merinta, an appliance infrastructure company, has closed up shop. Others are still in the hunt for developing a legitimate IA mass market, including Cidco, Inc., which had sold more than 70,000 of its MailStation "personal Internet communications products" by the end of 2000. Cidco then introduced two cordless e-mail appliances. One of these, the Mivo 350, displays text and graphics on a 16-grayscale LCD screen, supports HP DeskJet 600 and 900 series color inkjet printers, provides a photo album that lets users store up to 10 pictures for printing on the HP printers, and provides storage for up to 400 e-mails, 100 HTML pages, and 5 photos. The Mivo 350 also incorporates personalized Internet options such as local weather, news, stock quotes, horoscope, TV listings, and other features, delivered as HTML Web pages and reformatted to fit the Mivo 350 screen. Users can scroll up and down to view entire HTML pages, just as on a PC.

Heavyweights such as Compaq Computer and Microsoft are selling Compaq's iPaq Pocket PC, a PDA they promote as an IA device for accessing and eventually controlling communications-based Internet appliances. At the same time, Intel Corp. and Compaq are collaborating on the development of wireless handheld communications devices used to access and transmit data over the Internet, including IA applications. And Sony is promoting its eVilla Network Entertainment Center, saying that it offers "the best of the Internet without the hassles of a computer and gives you more entertainment and features than a standard Internet appliance." Samsung Electronics has also begun commercial installations of smart home appliances in a 100-apartment residential complex that is based on Echelon Corp.'s technology—essentially, a system that networks air conditioners, refrigerators, microwave ovens, and washing machines. Using a wireless Web pad, PC, or mobile phone, residents can control and monitor each device over the Internet, perform remote diagnostics, and check user guides.

Little has been heard from Nokia since early 2002 when it announced the formation of Nokia Home Communications, a new business unit it set up to develop Internet-based technology for the home. Japan's NEC Corp. has also yet to ship the 400 megabyte per second wireless transmission technology for networking home appliances that it announced in January 2000. (NEC's plans called for commercializing the device by the end of 2000.)

Networking giant Cisco Systems is working with Echelon, a control systems specialist, and Microsoft has licensed control technology from Intellon. Companies promoting Sun Microsystems' Java OS formed the Open Service Gateway initiative in 1999 to promote Java-based home networking, and virtually every manufacturer of home automation products has joined the Home API to develop application programming interfaces that would enable third-party software developers to create home-control programs based on the Microsoft Windows operating system.

That said, other issues will soon become apparent to well-informed consumers, particularly those early adopters with an interest in technology. One is the rapidly shrinking availability of Internet addresses. In theory at least, as pointed out earlier in this book, the current system will likely max out when it is hooked into 4.3 billion computers and other devices, or about twice the number currently assigned. With the continued growth of the Internet, and the introduction over the next few years of potentially millions of new, portable, Internet-enabled wireless devices, and the possibility of a totally new category of information appliances under development, with each of these or a tightly knit network of these appliances linked to the Internet, the problem starts to take shape. Most people who track these things anticipate that there will be several billion Internet-enabled devices in use in the world by 2006, but without the numeric address capability to support all of them.

There is something called Internet Protocol version 6 (IPv6), an upgrade of the current IPv4 technical standard, that is designed to handle the more than 4 billion new Internet addresses, but IPv6 may not be fully in place until at least 2006. Meanwhile, Internet use continues to grow, particularly outside North America.

Another thing: Should homeowners who buy information appliances worry about hackers, or anyone else, tapping into their Internet-linked refrigerators to look at its contents? (In this case, "only your doctor knows for sure" no longer applies.)

Want them or not, appliances will eventually be available with new, highly sophisticated features and functions, which—like those available in your VCR—you may never use.

TRUE STORY

About the time *2001: A Space Odyssey* was making its way to movie screens across the country, a computer programmer friend of mine, who also fancied himself a gourmet cook, was trying to use what he thought were artificial intelligence (AI) techniques—at least those that were available to him at the time—to create new recipes under very specific conditions. Convinced that you could not simply double the ingredients of a recipe for, say, four people, when you were expecting eight for dinner, and expect to get the same results, he attempted to write a computer program that would enable him to produce a recipe that would accurately match the original recipe in taste and texture, complete with a new set of ingredient levels and measures. He hoped to do this with virtually any dish he wanted to serve. He worked on this project for a long time, but he never could get it to work.

Home Networks and Home Automation

The amount of money spent by consumers on home networks and home automation in 1999 was probably only exceeded by the amount spent on ink and paper used in reporting on the potential growth in home networking and home automation in 1999.

Walter S. Mossberg, who started writing a personal technology column for the *Wall Street Journal* in 1991 when PCs were just beginning to use 3.5-inch floppy disks, had the industry tagged pretty well when he wrote, in May 1999, "Whenever the computer industry introduces a supposedly simple, purportedly must-have product, smart consumers should grow suspicious. This is an industry with a great hype machine but almost no clue about what mainstream users consider simple and what they really need. So skepticism is in order when considering the industry's latest 'hot' product: home networking systems." Two and a half years later, in October 2001, Mossberg wrote a much longer feature piece, an update on the "dramatic progress in personal technology," which he ended with the following warning: "While the PC has gotten easier, newer technologies, such as wireless home networking, are as depressingly complicated as computers once were." But this hasn't stopped new-home builders, hoping to differentiate their product, from developing and launching plans to install home networks in all the new homes they build in the next few years. The tough question for home builders and developers is, if they build it, will they come?

Projections for this market are all over the place. Market analysts at Cahners In-Stat say that more than 20 million homes in the United States have more than one PC. Allied Business Intelligence, another market research organization, says that by 2004, nearly 33% of U.S. households will have more than one computer. In January 2000, the research firm Strategic Analytics published a market study suggesting that consumers are lukewarm to home networking. Three months later, Cahners In-Stat, published its own market study in which it said that 2000 would be a big year for home networking. "Without a doubt," Cahners said, "this market will be extremely dynamic throughout 2000 as new products come to market and channel strategies are ironed out." Meanwhile, a survey by the Consumer Electronics Association (CEA), which has invested millions of dollars over the past two decades in home networking industry promotion and standards, indicated that most of these systems will *not* become commonplace in American homes. Most are too expensive for "average" consumers to comfortably afford and are typically best installed while a home is under construction, which immediately limits the market's growth. The trade association does, however, say that it sees a "groundswell of interest" in new home networking systems, with more than half of the consumers it surveyed expressing an interest in spending $5,000 for a network-enabling wiring system for a *new* home.

This is after years of developing and promoting a technical standard called the CEBus. According to the Consumer Electronics Association's CEBus Industry homepage, when traditional home electronic products are outfitted with "Home Plug & Play" network features, they can work together to offer a new generation of functionality. Some examples of the hype:

- Consumers could save on utility costs by having their homes automatically respond to variable time-of-day pricing by utility companies.
- Security systems could display a home's floor plan on a bedroom TV to troubleshoot problems as they happen.
- Household appliances could offer self-diagnostic options that notify when maintenance is due . . . and call to schedule a repairman's visit if so desired.
- Multitasking home PCs could monitor conversations between other household products and let the home's residents tell products what they want done.
- Household clocks could always keep the right time, even after power outages.
- Security system occupancy sensors could let the home's lighting and temperature control equipment know when the home or individual rooms are occupied.

Almost defensively, the CEBus Web asks: Haven't we heard this type of NEWS before?

Their answer is that "Prior announcements concerning standards and specifications for network products in homes differ significantly from the CEBus Industry Council's Home Plug & Play Specification. Prior standardization efforts asked manufacturers to adopt a message transportation method to get an application language (i.e., to get an appliance language, producers had to first select which horse was to carry the message)."

In January 2002, the Consumer Electronics Association announced that the Home Automation & Networking Association (HANA) had merged into the CEA, creating a new Home Automation & Networking (HAN) division for HANA's 500 members, including manufacturers and installers.

Of course, PCs are just a jumping-off point. Anyone can network his home entertainment system (including interactive

TVs and DVDs), home control system, and security system and link them to the Internet. Several homebuilders have developed an assortment of technology packages, from a basic wiring foundation to an "ultimate" networking system. According to the National Association of Home Builders, 34% of builders now offer so-called structured wiring packages as standard or optional amenities.

Every house now built in Las Vegas by Pulte Corp., the nation's largest homebuilder, includes a structured wiring system—one that basically lays a foundation for high-speed networking among a variety of devices within a home—with dual data/telephone cabling and dual RG-6 coaxial cabling run to every room jack. To accommodate home entertainment centers, family rooms feature as an option a special faceplate for four coaxial outlets and two RF-45 jacks. The larger faceplate is for video distribution, including closed-circuit TV. Empty plastic conduit installed from a point outside the home to each bedroom, home office area, and family room ensures the home can support any new technology. New cabling can be fished through the conduit if necessary.

Builders, developers, and new-home buyers in New Jersey can also now purchase in-home broadband networking from Verizon Wireless that will enable consumers to take advantage of the broadband Internet connections that are increasingly available.

But are homeowners really up to the task of installing a home network, particularly one that calls for integrating a PC with home control, security, and entertainment systems? In fact, are retailers able, or even willing, to take on the job of becoming facilities managers for home systems? Given some of the technical issues consumers and retailer/installers face, this is going to be a tough market to pitch.

One of the biggest hurdles in selling home networks has been the lack of a standard network protocol, which would allow a home system made up of components and devices from different manufacturers (sort of like a stereo system) to communicate with each other. Which means that several standards are currently in play and few, if any, of them interoperate.

In January 2001, the Consumer Electronics Association demonstrated its Versatile Home Network (VHN), which, for the technically inclined, operates at 400 megabits per second (400 Mb/s). At the same time, Silicon Image introduced its Digital Visual Interface (DVI), which can transmit at 5 gigabits per second (5 Gb/s). DVI has received high marks from several industry companies, including Universal Studios, Fox, and Warner Bros.

Most PC networks use one of two connectivity standards developed by competing consortia—HomeRF, a wireless system, or the HomePNA Phoneline Networking Alliance, which uses a home's existing telephone wiring. Both groups have developed protocols, or technical standards. More than 150 HomePNA-compliant networking products were on the market at the end of 2001; about 20 products were compliant with the HomeRF Shared Wireless Access Protocol (SWAP). A third home network that is moving into the marketplace uses the power line, but it is much slower than the other systems and only a few of these are available today. (Hoping to create a common power-line protocol, the Consumer Electronics Association formed what it calls the R7 Home Networking Committee, but several companies are not onboard. Shortly after the R7 was created, the HomePlug Powerline Alliance was launched by 3Com, Intel, Panasonic, Radio Shack, and others, to develop their own set of standards.)

HomeRF, with several heavyweight companies behind it, including IBM, Motorola, Compaq, Intel, Siemens, and Proxim, got a huge break in August 2001 when the FCC allowed the HomeRF Working Group to increase the transmission speed of SWAP to 10 Mbp/s, a fivefold increase in HomeRF bandwidth. The rule change, originally proposed by the HomeRF WG and its member companies, looked like it had significant implications for the growth of the home networking market. With this development, HomeRF WG member companies were now free to deliver a variety of new products supporting data speeds comparable to those of corporate wireless networks. With HomeRF running at 10 Mbp/s, consumers could now download Internet audio formats, including MP3, without interrupting other network activity. Dolby Labs said the FCC ruling would open up a new class of audio products that would include wireless surround speakers, high-quality networked digital jukeboxes, and Internet radios. The change also added new support for audio and video streaming and expanded the voice capabilities with support of up to eight cordless handsets.

Forget about it. HomeRF is already being overrun by another wireless network known as IEEE 802.11b, although another system—802.11a—is likely to give the "b" version a run for its money simply because it operates at a higher data rate. Developed primarily for use in offices and factories, 802.11 is gaining market ground on HomeRF fast enough that it could become the predominant in-home wireless system over the next few years.

How did this happen? For one thing, 802.11 network card prices have dropped tremendously—to within a few dollars of HomeRF adapters. The 802.11 technology is also being marketed much more aggressively than HomeRF, and it is increasingly being embedded into a variety of devices, such as laptop computers and wireless devices designed for the home, not simply designed to be plugged into them.

The cable industry also has a stake in home networking through CableLabs, cable operators' research and development consortium. More than a dozen companies, most of them the same companies that joined HomeRF, have signed on to this initiative, called CableHome. Each of them has agreed to work with a royalty-free pool. CableHome starts with the proposition that, if you choose to use home networking equipment approved by your cable operator, the operator will guarantee that it will work seamlessly with your broadband cable services delivered over cable.

Then there's Bluetooth, the short-range wireless system originally developed as a cable replacement between portable devices and fixed, wall-mounted access points. Bluetooth proponents see a huge opportunity in home networking in point-to-point and point-to-multipoint connections with several "piconets" linked together to allow continually flexible connections between portable devices and desktop PCs.

DSL Takes Its Hits

Like WAP, DSL has picked up a few nom de plumes of its own. Disappointing Subscriber Line and Digital Slow Line have shown up in letters to the editor of several industry magazines. But then, DSL—it actually stands for digital subscriber line and provides a high-speed connection to the Internet and corporate intranets—has been a big disappointment to millions who can't get DSL service, as well as to the millions who are getting it.

One consumer watchdog group, the New Networks Institute, estimates that as many as 75% of the DSLs have run into installation or service problems in some areas. But love it or hate it, DSL is the primary way most people get broadband access at home or in small offices. A survey of 150 readers of *Network Magazine* in 2001 indicated that most people hated it, with 55% reporting problems during installation and 35% declaring it a "major headache." Was the service delivered on time? Forty-seven percent said no. Thirty-two percent of the survey's respondents also said the speed of the service was less than advertised. The top rumor coming out of 2001 DSLcon, the industry's own trade show, reported *Telephony* magazine, was that "Technology has fallen victim to the hype machine." DSL even has its own Web sites to register complaints about DSL providers around the country—www.dslreports.com and www.2wire.com.

Despite the horror stories about installation problems, lack of access, and articles in the business press about independent DSL providers struggling to stay alive, market research continues to be generally positive, projecting that by 2003, DSL will exceed installations of all other broadband Internet access technologies combined, including leased lines, frame relay, ATM, cable modem, satellite, and wireless.

Others aren't so sure. DSL is a remote access technology that uses the existing telephone copper wiring infrastructure. It promises high bandwidth (meaning it's fast, at least 10 times faster than dial-up modems while leaving the phone line free for regular calls) and low cost—down to $20–$30 a month in some areas. It has another advantage to the user in that it is "always on," so there is no waiting for a modem to dial and connect before sending or receiving data. And there are no delays when a network connection is made, enabling DSL providers to use new Internet "push" technologies to send information to the subscriber's computer as soon as the information is available.

So, what's the problem? For one thing, customers must be within 10,000 to 18,000 feet of a central office to get the service. There are also aging copper networks to contend with. Industry estimates of the percentage of phone lines that can handle DSL range from 30% to 60%, which means the service may not be reliable. Installations often fail or simply won't work with some subscribers' wiring.

Another big hangup is that installation often requires working with at least three companies. It usually starts with buying the service from an Internet Service Provider, or ISP, which contracts with a DSP technology company to make the connection. The DSL specialist then must work with the local telephone company to handle some elements of the installation. DSL subscribers complain that when something doesn't work, these companies pass the blame and it can take weeks to fix the problem, if then. It's all about money. Several independent DSL providers have cancelled their expansion plans, revised earnings estimates, cut staff, or simply gone bankrupt.

One of the bankruptcy group, NorthPoint Communications, believes it was blindsided when Verizon Communications decided not to merge with NorthPoint, a deal that would have pumped $800 million into NorthPoint and kept its service intact. Another DSL provider, Rhythms NetConnections, was rumored to be making a bid for NorthPoint's customer base at approximately the same time that Rhythms hired investment banker Lazard Frere & Co. to look into its financial options, including the sale of the company. NorthPoint couldn't wait; it sold its equipment to AT&T. At about the same time, Excite At Home Corp., Microsoft, and Nippon Telegraph & Telephone's Verio business unit, which bought DSL access from North-Point, announced they were ending their DSL service, at least for the time being.

The big U.S. carriers, like SBC, the nation's leading DSL provider, Verizon, and some ISPs continue to push DSL as the best way to get homes and businesses connected. SBC hopes to hook up 80% of its customers to DSL by the end of 2002 through so-called neighborhood gateways—sort of subcentral telecom stations—to extend the currently limited reach of their central offices. Even technology hounds such as Stephen H. Wildstrom, *BusinessWeek's* technology columnist, are frustrated. "I'm disappointed," he wrote in December 2000, "but not surprised, to be stuck among the 95% or so of Americans without high-speed Internet service. Despite all the hype and talk of broadcast-type video and CD-quality audio over the Net, we are a dial-up nation, and we are likely to remain that way for a long time to come."

Still, DSL continues to sell well among consumers who need a high-speed alternative to their current dial-up service and are not price conscious. And it's strong internationally. Most analysts believe that DSL will continue to do well, particularly among consumers whose choice is between DSL and cable modems. They're competitively priced, and cable modems use the same type of wire that brings cable TV into the home; cable providers usually require that cable modem subscribers also sign up for the cable TV program service.

The cable guys also want to be your home network. Cable-Labs, mentioned earlier, has published several documents outlining specifications for quality of service and network architecture to be used when networking a cable connection in the home. The specs are part of the industry's effort to lay a technical groundwork to support home networking for the growing list of applications for the home and small offices, such as multimedia. It's also a clear attempt to better compete with DSL service providers. (Curiously, a study by the Strategis Group found that a greater percentage of cable modem users than DSL users are satisfied with their service based on several measures, including overall quality, access speed, and "always on" connectivity. The group also found that potential churn among DSL users—the rate at which people change or cancel their service—is nearly twice as high as that of cable modem users, 15% versus 8%. "Therefore," it says, "while DSL providers may acquire more customers due to their superior marketing efforts, they may eventually lose a higher percentage of customers to other DSL providers or to other access technologies than their cable modem counterparts."

When you can get it, and when it works, DSL can offer some interesting applications, like voice-over-DSL, high-speed Internet access, online gaming, video streaming, and conferencing. With more than 400 members, the DSL Forum is busily hyping cooperation among hardware and software vendors and service providers to enhance interoperability between different network's equipment, a move that will improve installation and cost effectiveness.

To help ease the pain of installation, DSL providers are pushing something called self-provisioning. That is, customers will be able to plug the DSL modem into an outlet and a phone line will configure itself by connecting and talking to the central office. The three-mile barrier is another problem, but the DSL camp thinks it may even have a way around that, with potential deployment of service up to five miles from a central office, possible in many areas. Meanwhile, new and emerging higher-speed versions of DSL, with longer range and improved performance, are in the works and may mean writing new technical standards. And at least five industry organizations, the DSL Forum, the Institute of Electrical and Electronics Engineers (IEEE), the Geneva-based International Telecommunications Union, the ATM Forum, and the American National Standards Institute (ANSI), are working the DSL standards issue.

The bigger problem is selling broadband, no matter what the technology, to consumers, particularly in a weakened economy and in an environment where most people use the Internet mainly to check their e-mail. Lower prices will help. So will an improved product and service.

Voice Recognition—So Much Talk

You may have seen the commercial in which a driver is approaching an intersection with a red light and he says,

"Green light" and the light immediately changes to green. Neat stuff, if it actually worked under real-life conditions.

This technology is known as voice recognition or speech recognition. It is the natural interface for wireless devices and one of the more obvious methods of easing concerns about drivers who become distracted while trying to punch in a number in those tiny keypads while using their cellphones. You can simply speak the name or number you want to call, either into a handheld phone or a well-placed microphone dedicated to this purpose.

Most of the time.

Several companies around the world have spent millions trying for at least 25 years to get this technology to work, but it still has some serious bugs. For one thing, it's often not very accurate; that is to say, the technology does not accurately recognize exactly what you're saying and respond accordingly. Another problem is ambient noise. Try using one of these systems at a noisy trade show, at an airport gate during a public address announcement, or in your car with the radio on.

Commercial products and services have been available for some time in some specific, well-controlled applications. Getting airline flight information is one that seems to work most of the time. Voice-activated consumer products are also available, but are technically limited.

Voice portal services such as BeVocal, ShopTalk, and Tellme Networks are gaining in popularity. Sprint PCS now offers its customers a service called Voice Command, which enables users to create a voice-accessible address book. Yahoo! and Lycos have introduced a suite of speech tools and services that give consumers access to their content by telephone. Lernout & Hauspie, a leading speech technology company until it entered bankruptcy proceedings and then closed up shop, had announced plans to enter the wireless communications market with a system that lets mobile phone users access information on the Web, such as traffic reports and movie listings. PDA maker Palm has teamed with SpeechWorks International to add speech recognition to Palm's Web-based calendar service. Motorola has introduced its iRadio Internet system for automobiles with Internet access, a directory dialer, and address book, and the ability to send and receive e-mail through its voice recognition feature. All of these efforts should lead to improved voice recognition services.

Like so many other technologies, the Internet will be the driving force behind getting voice access into the network. Increasingly, the technology, because it is so easy to use, actually presents carriers and other wireless service providers with an attractive alternative to existing industry technology standards such as the Wireless Application Protocol (WAP). As an alternative to WAP, speech-recognition enables users to access Internet content hands-free.

One of the first things that has to happen to make voice recognition work for everyone is the creation of a technical standard, and that process is well underway. Version 1.0 of the VoiceXML (Voice eXtensible Markup Language) specification has been accepted as a standard by the World Wide Web Consortium (W3C). The W3C's Voice Browser Working Group has agreed to base its efforts to develop a standard on VoiceXML. This is a spec that could provide a high-level programming interface to speech and telephony resources for application developers, service providers, and equipment manufacturers.

Unfortunately, more than two years after Motorola, IBM, Lucent Technologies, and AT&T helped form the VoiceXML Forum to bring technical standards to voice recognition, there is still no way of ensuring that any of these systems can talk to each other.

Interoperability concerns have begun to slip through the standards development cracks and have taken on more of a competitive marketing track, with voice recognition companies introducing their own "open standard" systems and selling their products as modules that can be updated or changed-out as new accessories and technologies are developed. The result is that few of these products may work together, or they won't work together very well.

Wireless service providers can't wait for these developments to kick in. They're convinced that easy access to different services through voice recognition will increase their traffic—and their revenues. Automated speech-recognition-enabled services could also produce cost savings for the carriers; the cost of processing a phone call using an automated directory assistant is about one-tenth the cost of processing the same call using operator assistance. Bottom line, look for voice portal companies to introduce more sophisticated and useful applications. In fact, voice access to e-mail and Web-based information and services appears to be well on its way to becoming a primary consumer interface for a variety of portable electronic products, including electronic games.

A Cry for Help

With more than 118,000 calls a day made in the United States to 911 and other emergency numbers from wireless phones, the Federal Communications Commission thought it might be a good idea to make it easier to determine the location of people making an emergency call—even if they don't have a clue where they are. From this, Enhanced 911, or E-911, was born.

The media picked up on this early with a story of a New Jersey family that ran off the road in the middle of Nebraska late at night without knowing where they were. They called E-911 and the system tracked them to within a few hundred meters and sent help. Technology to the rescue . . . again.

But what technology? Nearly every major U.S. carrier has filed a request for an extension with the FCC, claiming the technology wasn't up to the task. At least not under the tight location restrictions required by the commission.

The current E-911 rules were adopted in 1996 and reflected the technology available at the time, which anticipated only a network-based approach called automatic location identification (ALI). Now, with the FCC's E-911 plan fully envisioned, emergency response centers can locate the caller by using the nearest cellular towers to triangulate the call and determine which tower is generating the strongest signal from the emergency call. But then the FCC revised its rules to make room for other options.

Under the new rules, wireless carriers who employ a location technology with new, modified, or upgraded cellphones were required to begin activating and selling them no later than March 1, 2001. At least half of these handsets were to be ALI-capable no later than October 1, 2001. Also, at least 95% of all new digital phones were to be ALI-enabled and activated for this service no later than October 1, 2002.

For network-based E-911 to work, the revised FCC rules call for carriers to achieve 100-meter accuracy for 67% of mobile emergency calls and 300-meter accuracy for 95% of all of these calls. Carriers going the handset route, which means they will use the satellite-based Global Positioning System (GPS), which is more accurate and more reliable, must demonstrate an accuracy of 50 meters for 67% of its emergency calls and 150 meters for 95% of these calls.

Several carriers, including ALLTEL, U.S. Cellular, and Nextel Communications, informed the FCC early on in the process that they were opting for a handset-based E-911 system. Others, including Verizon Wireless and Western Wireless, for example, opted for the network-based system. But they have other technology choices. Most of the carriers selecting the network option favored a combination of something called time difference of arrival (TDOA), which calculates a phone's position based on the speed the signal reaches multiple nearby antennas, and angle of arrival (AOA). With AOA, cellular towers identify the direction from which a signal is coming and then pilots the direction of the incoming call based on a reading from two towers. AT&T Wireless and VoiceStream announced plans early to adopt another hybrid system known as enhanced observed time difference (EOTD). The major supplier of EOTD technology, which works only with cellphones or other wireless devices based on the European-developed digital Global System for Mobile Communications (GSM) system, is U.K.-based Cambridge Positioning Systems. CPS's Cursor software does not require any hardware modification to the handset, only some low-level reprogramming and sufficient memory.

The advantage of using GPS-equipped cellphones is that it gives carriers a running start on providing its customers with a wide array of location-based services. These include navigation data (including directions and information on nearby restaurants and retail outlets), traffic and weather reports, and a wide range of regional entertainment options.

As far as the law enforcement and other emergency services agencies are concerned, the carriers aren't moving fast enough. The Association of Public-Safety Communications Officials (APCO) punched out news releases for months on vehicular deaths across the country that it said might have been avoided if the caller's location could have been determined by E-911 technology.

At this point, it's just a matter of time. Eventually, everyone will have a portable phone with access to some kind of E-911 capability. The fear is that with wireless carriers pushing for new revenue-generating, location-based services, someone responding to an accident might be sent to a drug store on the next block.

When Technology "Push" Comes To Shove

The Insurance Institute for Highway Safety gave the Jeep Liberty a "poor" rating in 2001 because it fared the worst in a rear-end collision test. Much of the damage resulted from a simple design choice made by Jeep, which attached the spare tire to the back of the vehicle, making it swerve, according to the Institute. Jeep said it mounted the tire in the back to create more room inside for storage. "That's what our customers want," a Jeep spokesman said.

Manufacturers, like Jeep's parent, DaimlerChrysler, like to think they're in the loop because they conduct focus groups and surveys and receive a certain amount of feedback from their sales agencies. In turn, consumers think they influence the design and *development of new products based on their input—for example, what they buy and what they tell car salesmen.*

When it comes to technology, it usually works a little differently. Car manufacturers want to introduce new features, particularly as technologies advance and become available at a reasonable cost. (The remote control key, digital displays, and in-vehicle navigation are pretty good examples.) Technology adds value to manufacturers' products; it's also a competitive issue. But, since most consumers know so little about technology and what the manufacturer can actually produce, the market research has limited value. More often than not, the end-product is simply a result of the available technology and the cost to take that technology to market. Product differentiation is important but very difficult to achieve. In fact, it's rare. So, there is a balancing act in attempting to match new products with technological advancements and consumers' perceived value and, to a lesser extent, requirements. This is where manufacturers get into what they call "push" and "pull" strategies.

• • •

Most innovations require a technology "push" to get new products to market and to start promoting them. This is obviously true in technologies that are totally new and initially transparent to the consumer. The market "pull" scenario usually more closely involves the consumer. Europe's Short Messaging Service (SMS) is a reasonably good example. Although SMS carriers are "pushing" information to its subscribers, such as sports scores and stock quotes, many SMS users have requested specific, even customized, information through their devices. Many of them are even willing to pay for this service. While pushing is often more challenging for manufacturers and service providers who must constantly introduce new technologies and services, pulling is where the action is.

It really doesn't really matter whether you like or dislike technology. One way or another, you're going pay for it, even if you don't use it. (Tucker Eskew, a senior advisor to George W. Bush during the presidential campaign of 2000, may have gone a little overboard when, referring to Vice President Al Gore's always-handy Palm, he said, "We will not pander to the tech community by strapping a PDA to his [Bush's] waist.")

Nearly 30 years after the first VCR was introduced by Sony, VCRs can be found in 91% of all U.S. households. But even today, few consumers take advantage of all of the features of one of their most prized consumer electronics products. This is not unusual, according to the Consumer Electronics Association's Market Research Department. While the CEA says it has never actually asked its member companies or consumers how much they use the functionality of their video, audio, mobile electronics, and other communications and information technology and accessory products, its educated guess is less than 30%. Most industry analysts think it's a lot less.

The Conference Board, which creates and disseminates information about management and the marketplace, says the key to the future success of the U.S. economy is using new technologies, not producing them. In a report on information and communications technologies (ICT) published in October 2001, Dr. Bart van Ark, a consulting director for The Conference Board's International Economic Research, wrote, "It is the use of ICT, not its production, that is the likely key to future growth acceleration. Even though computer and communications equipment have been readily available in a worldwide market for quite some time, it appears that we are at the beginning, not the end, of the diffusion process, even in the United States. This suggests that the longer-run productivity gains and market advantages are likely to be found in the creative use of information and communications technologies. While the relative size of the information and communications technology-using sectors is similar across countries," van Ark says, "there are substantial differences in the productivity growth resulting from investments in information and communications technologies." In the United States, according to The Conference Board, 1.1% of the acceleration in labor productivity growth from 1995 to 1999 arose from intensive information and communications technology users, on top of the 0.35% from information and communication technology producers. In the second half of the '90s, the United States greatly benefited from information and communications technology production and use in speeding up its productivity growth.

How much technology will consumers accept? Will they buy into ads from yet another medium they don't want? Surveys indicate that they will if the product or service being advertised is free or if it is being offered at a huge discount. Under these circumstances, they say they will "opt in," or accept "pushed" messages that, for example, remind them that it's still early in the day and there's a Starbucks just three blocks down the road. Otherwise, forget about it. The "pull" model that enables you to find the nearest Chinese restaurant or helps you locate an ATM—but only if you request this information—is still more acceptable to most people, certainly to most Americans. Accenture found that only about one-quarter of the 2,300 wireless device owners it surveyed in the United States and United Kingdom were able to receive messages from retailers, and most of these proved to be annoying and intrusive.

Still, there may be no escaping these ads. Analysts project that by 2003, more Americans will access the Internet from their cellphones than from their PCs. One way that's going to happen is for carriers to offer certain services without charge. (They will, however, charge the messenger.) Even if you innocently check out one of the wireless messages provided for the more than 200 corporate clients of ShareSpan, you are going to get an ad at the bottom of the screen—something like, "Go to Mercedes.com." That's how they pay the bills and keep the messaging service free.

Mobile Commerce Becomes a Tough Sell

If there was ever an example of push coming to shove, it's in mobile commerce. M-commerce is pretty much the same thing as electronic (or "e") commerce, except that it operates in a mobile "buy on the fly" environment.

M-commerce is probably still misunderstood by those who think they understand it, but that hasn't slowed the hype. Revenue projections for m-commerce range into the billions of dollars. But this will only happen, we're told, if the wireless industry properly promotes wider content and service development. Unfortunately, surveys by the Consumer Electronics Association send a strong message that while American consumers want content, they don't want to pay for it. Europeans are a little more flexible. Japanese consumers don't particularly like being "pushed," but they will accept personalized pushed content; that is, information on things of interest to them personally, such as a sale at a favorite shop they may be approaching, either in their car or on foot.

Market research firm The Yankee Group puts m-commerce in three categories—premium content, remote payment, and point-of-sale (POS) applications. Premium content is expected to be big, especially in Europe, accounting for up to 75% of m-commerce transactions by 2006. Remote payment is a work in progress and will take time to develop as consumers figure it out and become convinced that any personal transactions they conduct remotely (that is, wirelessly) will be secure. POS is one of those opportunities that will kick in with the help of early adopters and then begin to spread, with teenagers and young adults accounting for a large percentage of POS activity.

Another research organization, Meta Group, has its own list of concerns for m-commerce. Meta believes that the three industries most likely to support m-commerce may be off worrying about other things. The travel industry, for example, while a leading innovator in mobile computing, has to be thinking about how it's going to survive over the next few years. Banks continue to develop new wireless services, but will this be enough to promote m-commerce and pick up some of the slack in the travel market? Telecommunications companies, the third element cited by Meta, also may not be able or willing to fund m-commerce developments in the near term.

What's an Industry to Do?

As 2000 came to a close, m-commerce looked hot. That view continued into 2001 when several market research houses and other analysts suggested in published reports that by the end of 2002, at least half the owners of Internet-enabled mobile devices would be using them for shopping and banking. M-commerce began to lose its "next big thing" luster after several analysts updated their surveys and started sharing the results with their press and media contacts. Here are some of the more prominent headlines that appeared in the second half of 2001, and their sources:

- "M-Commerce: Hype or a Real Business Opportunity" (Zona Research)
- "Study Calls M-Commerce Predictions 'Hype'" (Cahners In-Stat Group)
- "Overly Hyped M-Commerce Won't Take Off Until 2004" (The Strategis Group)
- "Post-PC Platforms Offer Limited Advertising Opportunities, Despite Enormous Hype" (Jupiter Media Metrix)
- "Study: M-Commerce Hype Exceeds Reality" (Frost & Sullivan)
- "Study: M-Commerce Launched Too Early" (Cahners In-Stat Group)
- "M-Commerce Users Feel Frustrated" (The Boston Consulting Group)
- "Study Shows Consumers Aren't Ready for Mobile Commerce" (A. T. Kearney)
- "Disinterest Snags Mobile Commerce" (Jupiter Media Metrix)
- "M-Commerce Hype and Reality" (Column in *Wireless Week* by James Green, CEO of Giant Bear, Inc.)

Can m-commerce survive the hype? There is every indication that consumers have no or little interest in buying anything on their Web-enabled phones or PDAs. At least, not yet. In fact, much of the early news and analysis surrounding the potential revenue that could be generated from m-commerce was simply misleading. Most consumers surveyed said they simply have no need to use the wireless Internet to make purchases. Many said it is too difficult (tech geeks notwithstanding). Others expressed their concern about security.

Several analysts now believe that wireless carriers and wireless device manufacturers failed to consider the gap between what the technology can do today and what consumers have been led to expect. Difficult and unwieldy interfaces—the cramped keyboards used to enter data into a wireless device and the tiny displays—and the high cost of the device and service, along with painfully slow transmission speeds (particularly when compared to what people are used to on their desktop PCs), will improve, but not dramatically, and not anytime soon.

Wide-ranging market forecasts for m-commerce from several independent research organizations—from $700 million to $27 billion in 2004—haven't helped instill confidence in the category. Internet statistics provider NewsFactor.com says, "Maybe the 'm' in m-commerce should stand for 'minor,' 'miniscule,' or 'marginal.'" Emarketer has conservatively projected that 30 million m-commerce users spending $50 each will buy $1.5 billion in goods, services, and applications using mobile devices in 2004. Emarketer says, "M-commerce will either kick in by the end of 2002 with carriers driving new wireless data and Internet services, or it will fall further behind Europe and Asia and wallow in a mire of competing technology platforms." Datamonitor's survey found that two-thirds of the more than 300 European companies it quizzed in mid-2000 had implemented or planned to implement an m-commerce system. The others said they were skeptical about investing in m-commerce systems. (In Britain, 46% of the respondents said they were skeptical; in Italy, it was 45%.)

Baby Steps

Part of the problem is that m-commerce is still in its infancy. So much so that some people haven't even heard of it. There is also still some disagreement about what it actually is or what it might become. The biggest challenge at the moment is convincing end-users that m-commerce is a complement to e-commerce and not a substitute.

There are still many issues to be worked out, like trying to figure out what consumers will buy using their portable wireless devices. Most likely, it won't be cars, houses, refrigerators, or other so-called high-ticket items. These require extensive research by serious shoppers and are more likely to be checked out and purchased from a desktop PC. Even ordering flowers or a rental car from a cellphone or a wireless PDA continues to haunt the technically challenged.

What does that leave? Actually, a lot. Entertainment (buying tickets to movies and concerts, purely as a convenience or as an impulse buy), stock trading, personal banking (expect wireless ATM access to be ubiquitous), and travel (changing your plans when necessary) are all logical and even potentially strong candidates for m-commerce activity. Fidelity Investments' 10 million retirement plan investors can now use their wireless devices to conduct transactions over the Internet. You can also check on nearby restaurants at lunchtime and shops when you need something and you're not familiar with the area.

Several hundred wireless-enabled parking meters have been installed in Leichardt, Australia, to test how they work with Short Message Service (SMS) or voice commands using wireless devices. One of the more useful features of the field test is that users can receive alerts when their meter is running out of time and automatically—and wirelessly—recharge the meter. European soft drink vendors have also been testing wireless electronic payment systems on soda and candy machines, using cellphones and wireless-enabled PDAs. It is going to take time before any of these things are commonplace, which may explain why Cahners In-Stat titled one of its market studies, published in July 2001, "Mobile Commerce: A Work In Progress."

Most people like to shop, but will they do it from their cellphones? How can the wireless carriers make money on m-commerce? T-Mobile, the wireless carrier arm of Germany's Deutsche Telecom, says that fewer than 1% of its subscribers access the Internet, and then only once or twice a month. Will consumers use their wireless devices for m-commerce? (Charles Schwab Corp., the largest online brokerage, which spent millions creating a 60-person wireless division, disclosed that less than 0.1% of online trading was made on wireless devices in 2000.) How will consumers pay for m-commerce purchases? How secure are wireless payments? Whether people can safely key their credit card and pin numbers into a wireless device is a legitimate question. What about privacy? (Sprint PCS routinely embeds customers' phone numbers in Web page requests.) Will they accept advertising that is "pushed" to them through their cellphones and PDAs? How much useful information can be displayed on tiny cellphone screens?

As already indicated, m-commerce is also a cultural issue. A lot more Americans own desktop PCs than do Europeans, Asians, or Latin Americans, making it easier for them to search for and buy products and services at home or at work. On the other hand, marketers everywhere know that teenagers and young adults are the most likely candidates to use new technologies, and that squares nicely with recent data showing that the number of wireless users under 18 years old has exploded from an estimated 5% in 1999 to 23% in 2000.

M-commerce is also a tough sell for the information technology (IT) community. Like the Internet, it will be a whole new thing for many IT managers. And it's expensive, making it hard to justify, certainly in the early stages. What kind of support are they going to get from corporate management, particularly when they determine what it's going to cost the organization to standardize on specific wireless platforms and build their own corporate mobile infrastructure? How will employees who already own and use mobile products and services take to their IT department's efforts to move to a corporate-wide mobile technology standard?

Wireless Advertising

The hype surrounding mobile advertising, a key component of m-commerce, "far exceeds" the reality of what is actually happening, Frost & Sullivan discovered in its study of the market early in 2001. The reality, according to several other surveys conducted about the same time, suggest that advertisers will be slow to allocate dollars for campaigns on post-PC technologies as they struggle to control the key benefits of advertising on wireless devices. Based on its "executive survey," Jupiter Media Metrix says marketers that believe they can overcome the limitations of interactive and wireless devices as branding vehicles are missing the point. To maximize ad campaigns on these devices, advertisers must isolate and understand the attributes of modal targets—that is, distinct groups of individuals with similar behaviors and attitudes who use Internet-enabled devices—and match the marketing message to the objectives of the consumer using the device, not to their demographic profiles. "Post-PC opportunities," says Jupiter, "are a need-to-have for a few categories of advertisers and only a nice-to-have for most."

With that kind of data, the advertising community decided that it needed a new trade group to pitch its story. The Wireless Advertising Association (WAA) was formed as an independent unit of the Internet Advertising Bureau (IAB), which was formed by the merger of the Wireless Advertising Industry Association (WAIA) and the IAB's Wireless Ad Council (WAC). In an effort to define a policy that will help the industry police itself, the WAA says it does not condone wireless push advertising or condone content intentionally or negligently sent to any subscriber's wireless device without explicit subscriber permission and clear identification of the sender. The development of this policy comes after what the WAA says is its recognition of "the considerable experience of Internet advertisers and marketers, particularly those engaged in permission e-mail campaigns." The WAA defines push advertising or content as any content sent by or on behalf of advertisers and marketers to a wireless device at a time other than when the subscriber initiates a request.

Under WAA guidelines, advertisers and marketers shall not send wireless push ads or content to a subscriber's wireless device unless the subscriber "opts in," or give specific permission to receive this content. This includes but is not limited to audio, Short Messaging Service (SMS), e-mail, multimedia messaging, cell broadcast, picture messages, pushed content (as opposed to content solicited by the wireless subscriber), or any other pushed advertising or other content. Moreover, subscriber permission for wireless push ads must be verified through what it calls Confirmed Opt-In. The WAA expects Confirmed Opt-In to be the baseline for wireless subscriber permission.

Jupiter Media Metrix has offered several suggestions to get around the hype and make m-commerce work. One is that wireless carriers should create free, dedicated shopping channels on their wireless Web portals while merchants offer discounts or promotions to consumers making their first purchases over the wireless Web. "Mobile commerce is about influencing purchases, not transactions," says Jupiter. "The greatest area of promise for mobile commerce is to bridge the gap between the touch and feel physical world and the convenient and cost competitive online world: merchants that understand and act on the 'mobile bridge' concept."

Influencing mobile users with promotions based on timely, personalized, and location-based research will be the key to successful m-commerce.

Location, Location, Location

If you're walking through Times Square for the first time and you suddenly have a craving for a roast beef sandwich on rye, maybe a big pickle on the side, and a cream soda, you may be able to find a deli within walking distance by consulting your Internet-enabled cellphone or PDA. This, in its simplest form, is what is now widely referred to as a location-based service (LBS), and it represents an important part of m-commerce. But with so many issues still in flux (security, roaming, standards, and technical integration) and with no proven business model, most wireless carriers are afraid to pioneer these services. Despite early signs of opportunity as a new source of revenue and some heady independent market projections, wireless carriers have come to view LBS as a costly add-on to their networks. In fact, they haven't really figured out how to make money with this emerging technology. Equipment manufacturers, on the other hand, can't wait.

Motorola, for one, has formed an alliance with MapInfo Corp., to provide MapInfo's miGuide, a location-based service that delivers maps and driving directions on Motorola's Java technology-enabled handsets. This includes Yellow Pages and retail business locations. Trimble Navigation, whose portable, satellite-based Global Positioning Systems (GPS) helped U.S. troops find their way in a featureless desert during the Persian Gulf War, has formed Trimble Information Services to offer Internet location-based services to businesses that need help managing their fleet of vehicles, and to consumers with location-enabled mobile devices. Garmin Ltd., another navigation specialist, has introduced eMap, a handheld electronic map/GPS with the ability to locate addresses and points of interest, such as hotels and restaurants.

The GSM Association, the body that supports the European-developed Global System for Mobile Communications (GSM), which accounts for about 70% of the global digital cellular wireless market, has also jumped into the m-commerce picture, creating the Mobile Services Initiative, or M-Services, to enhance the benefits to consumers using GSM handsets by delivering a globally available set of services through the mobile Internet. (Hoping to better understand how wireless technologies can drive consumers into their stores, four major United Kingdom retail chains—HMV, Lush, Oddbins, and Superdrug—are using location-based targeted marketing, enabling consumers to key in a store location on their GSM-based wireless devices to "browse" promotions.)

New GSM services could include enhanced graphics, music, video, games, customized ring tones, and screen savers. Manufacturers such as Motorola, Ericsson, Nokia, Alcatel, Samsung, and Siemens have come out in support of the M-Services initiative. Several, mostly European, wireless carriers have also joined the M-Services effort.

Other industry companies have formed alliances to help kick-start their own m-commerce programs. But they may have to watch out for government regulators. What, for example, is the outlook for new vehicle location-based technologies when it's already illegal in many municipalities and New York State to use your cellular phone while driving?

Telematics Downshifts

Telematics is another word to add to your vocabulary and another key element to m-commerce. It's one of those you're-going-to-get-it-whether-you-want-it-or-not developments. And it's going to be foisted on everyone who buys a new car over the next few years, especially if it's a "luxury" model.

Automobile manufacturers, like their consumer electronics counterparts, are big on "value added" features, and telematics fits this category almost perfectly. Telematics not only adds value to their products, it helps differentiate their vehicles—style, color, price, and model type notwithstanding.

Telematics, which is essentially the integration of mobile communications and information technologies into car and trucks, includes such features as satellite-based Global Positioning System (GPS) navigation (usually with location-based commercial services), 100-channel satellite radios, ceiling-mounted DVDs, MP3 players, and in-dash CD players with hundreds of songs compressed into a built-in memory package, interactive video with downloadable games, and safety and security features such as a front-seat video display that switches to a closed-circuit camera for checking what's behind you when the parking brake is disengaged. Also included are vehicle communications (cellular, two-way radio, two-way messaging) and monitoring (wireless telemetry or other short-range radio technologies to monitor vehicle functions, such as tire pressure).

Calculators are a good example of how the value-added system works. The prices of the earliest four-function calculators (add, subtract, multiply, and divide) dropped precipitously, largely because of the competition. At one time, there were 82 "pocket calculator" brands. The price-cutting cut deeply into manufacturers' profit margins. But they quickly upgraded their calculators with much more functionality and introduced "scientific" calculators, which eventually led to the demise of engineers' slide rules.

Adding value to the new calculators enabled manufacturers and retailers to charge more for them, making up for the hit they took on their lower-end "loss leader" models. In time—and it didn't take long—calculators became a mass market item. Just about everyone had a calculator; some people had several. Economies of scale quickly took over. Similarly, automakers start out by offering their newest features in only their top-of-the-line models and then begin to provide them as "standard" features in all of their models. Like a VCR, whether you use all of its features or not, you're paying the price. The equipment side of telematics is growing because automakers are putting it into cars, not because people are asking for it.

J.D. Powers Associates, which regularly surveys several aspects of the auto industry, including who likes or dislikes what in their vehicles, has already determined that most consumers are not very impressed with the new in-vehicle technology they have seen so far. Small screen maps scored poorly in a J. D. Powers survey. So did non-DVD-based mapping systems with limited geographic coverage. In fact, while navigation systems are of interest to consumers, the demand for these devices lags well behind consumers' interest in more mundane safety features, such as side-impact air bags and daytime running lights.

Want it or not, by the middle of 2001, there were more than 135,000 factory-installed navigation systems in 26 different late-model U.S. vehicles, up from 25,000 in seven different 1998 model U.S. cars. A Telematics Research Group study indicates that by 2006, 33% of new autos will have a factory-installed telematic system of some kind. That amounts to an installed base of nearly 21 million telematics-enabled vehicles in the United States.

Just about everyone is onboard. Motorola formed the Automotive Communications & Electronics Systems Group just to beef up its telematics activities. Ericsson has joined with Magneti Mareli, a leading designer and developer of telematics systems in Europe, to develop mobile Internet applications. Microsoft has demonstrated its Car.NET technology, which enables mobile device users to shuttle information between their cars, home, and office. Novatel Wireless is expanding its vehicle tracking and fleet management program. Subaru of America is collaborating with General Motors' OnStar and expects to add telematics to its 2003 Outback. Ford has created a joint venture operation, called Wingcast, with wireless systems developer Qualcomm in an attempt to match the success of OnStar. (Launched in 1996, OnStar claims its system, which does everything from enabling drivers to make and receive hands-free, voice-activated calls to accessing personalized Web-based information in a hands-free-voice-activated manner, is now in more than 1.3 million vehicles.) Toyota is developing what it calls the G-Book service, through which drivers will use emerging Third-

Generation cellular networks to download road maps and send and receive e-mail, as well as receive music, news, stock prices, and traffic and weather reports.

Ford also plans to sell Cellport Systems' universal docking station as a factory-installed option or aftermarket device. This development is potentially significant because it could settle the argument over whether consumers will insist on using their own privately purchased cellphones to use anywhere—including in their cars or trucks—or whether they will opt for a permanently installed cellphone that is specifically engineered for the vehicle in which it is mounted. Engineers are pitching the latter, stressing that phones can be developed for a specific environment that will optimize the use of voice-recognition technology, which could take the edge off the growing push for banning cellphone use while driving.

The numbers also favor specially designed, factory-installed systems. A survey conducted by the U.S. Department of Transportation's National Highway Traffic Safety Administration (NHTSA) estimates that 500,000 drivers of passenger vehicles are talking on handheld cellphones at any given moment.

Cellphone manufacturers aren't very high on factory-installed systems, preferring to have their customers trade in their phones for new models every 18 months or so. Since voice-recognition systems still have not done a very good job of operating with a great deal of accuracy (they often don't work well with a lot of background noise), the betting is that personally owned, portable cellphones will continue to be the way of the world. Or, at least, of the United States.

Down the Road

Down the road, car dealers are looking for ways to conduct remote diagnostics on the vehicles they sell. They want to remotely monitor the vehicle's performance and alert their customers to problems before they actually occur. Several wireless carriers, telematics service providers, and application, content, and system developers have formed an industry consortium—the Mobile and Automotive Geographic Information Core (MAGIC)—to make remote diagnostics happen through the development of open industry technical standards for telematics and related location-based devices and services.

The Consumer Electronics Association's Mobile Electronics Standards Committee is also working with the Society of Automotive Engineers (SAE) and automakers to develop plug-and-play consumer connections to in-vehicle networks that allow devices to share resources and exchange information. The SAE, through its SAE Strategic Alliance, is also working with the Alliance of Automobile Manufacturers to figure out ways to reduce or eliminate driver distractions.

At some point, drivers will have access to voice-activated and controlled games and a universal vehicle identification system that allows drivers to zip through tollbooths anywhere in the country.

So much for cupholders.

GPS—The Sky's the Limit

Like the aircraft and shipping industries operating around the world, most mobile commerce and telematics systems operating in the United States, Europe, and Japan must rely on the U.S. Department of Defense owned-and-operated Global Positioning System (GPS). After the cellphone, GPS may turn out to be the most important piece of electronic equipment in any vehicle.

Initiated as a test program by the Pentagon in the early 1970s, the GPS has provided position location service for military and civilian applications since 1992, including recreational users such as boat owners, fisherman, campers, and hikers and, more recently, for in-vehicle navigation. (Even before the DoD could get with the program, families in the United States were buying up handheld GPS systems during the Persian Gulf War and sending them to their sons in the war zone so they could know their specific location in the Iraqi desert.) Portable or vehicle-mounted GPS devices receive signals from the satellites and calculate the user's position to within about 100 yards for most civilian GPS systems and even closer with military GPS devices.

GPS operates a 24-satellite network 24 hours a day. It serves an unlimited number of users and operates in all weather conditions. To enhance its accuracy so that drivers know what intersection to turn at in a big city in which the GPS signal may be shielded by tall buildings, dead reckoning is sometimes used with GPS. This is a technique by which vehicle location can be matched to onboard maps by calculation of the distance traveled from a specific starting point.

GPS-based car navigation systems have been in use in Japan for more than 10 years, but Japan is working on developing its own system. Europe reluctantly uses GPS because it is the only satellite-based navigation game in town, but it has always been uncomfortable about using a system that is operated and controlled by the Pentagon. With that in mind, the European Geostationary Navigation Overlay Service, known as the Galileo program, has been under development for several years at an anticipated cost of $3.16 billion. Meanwhile, Russia also operates a 24-satellite system, the Global Navigation Satellite System (GLONASS), but it has never technically measured up to the DoD's GPS. In fact, barely half of the GLONASS satellites are ever in full operation at any one time.

TRUE STORY

Some years ago, during a coffee break at an all-day technology briefing sponsored by Motorola, I got into a conversation with the director of marketing for the company's navigation products.

As the break was wrapping up, we exchanged business cards. His card had all the usual stuff on it—the bold, black Motorola logo, his name and title, address, phone and fax numbers, and his cellphone number. No e-mail address; this was in the pre-e-mail era. But there was one item on his card that I had never seen before: the coordinates—the longitude and latitude—for his office.

Wow! I thought, this is great. Not only does it serve as a sort of subliminal (but clever) promotional device, but it provides a very practical piece of data, especially if you have a GPS.

"Now you have no excuse for not finding my office," he said.

"Not only that," I was quick to add, "I can put a missile through your window."

The Data Game

There are few stronger influences on high-tech markets than traditional independent market research. In the interest of intellectual honesty, most market research organizations should stamp the covers of their studies and reports with "The hype starts here."

Unlike weather forecasters, who have enough trouble producing accurate five-day forecasts, market research analysts are usually thinking in five-year terms, which means they have a significant impact on the development of business models and corporate plans, including capital investments and venture capital activities, even the stock market, simply by how they project and analyze future markets.

It's an even trickier deal for journalists who often get an idea for a story based primarily on some impressive (and often outlandish) numbers in a published market research report. (One of these firms, Forrester Research, claims it gets about 2,000 press calls a month.) They then find themselves justifying the piece with data from the research, usually in the first few paragraphs of the feature. Which came first, the data, which generates the idea for the piece and helped the writer sell the idea to his or her editor, or the idea for the story, which is supported by the market data?

Data from high-tech studies are also used in the promotional material of magazines to help justify features related to the studies in upcoming issues. PR agencies often place contact lists of favored analysts in their clients' press kits (obviously, those that speak well of their clients or the client's industries). Market analysts who appear at technology seminars and industry conferences play a big, although often subliminal, role in hyping new and emerging technologies, partly because their presentations are mostly very positive, and these are often woven into press reports of the conference.

Where it gets tricky is that little is done to encourage or monitor the objectivity of most analysts. Some of them, for example, have authored reports paid for by their clients, and these reports are published under the analyst company's name and are used as marketing material by the client. Some analysts own stock in the companies or industries they are analyzing. Many of them speak at seminars sponsored by vendors they cover in their research. They're also often called on to give presentations at press conferences sponsored by vendors and trade associations. At the end of the day (or, more accurately, the end of a five-year projection), there is little, if any, reporting on the accuracy of their market projections or analysis.

Indeed, how accurate are these reports? Studies made a few years ago projecting the widespread use of Web-based features in wireless devices were totally off the mark. Market research suggested a "massive" push behind the use of the Wireless Application Protocol (WAP) to access the Internet through wireless devices in 2001, but it never materialized. A number of projections of the Internet appliance and mobile commerce markets contradicted each other, even when these markets were showing little evidence of where they were going and how they might actually develop.

With m-commerce, a market in which very few people have any experience, analysts are going through a difficult learning curve. In November 2000, despite high hopes and plenty of hype, The Boston Consulting Group found that one in five mobile device users in the United States had stopped using m-commerce after a few attempts. Consumers said their experience simply didn't live up to their expectations. A few months later, in January 2001, a survey published by Telphia reported that about 25% of those who access the Internet with wireless mobile devices have purchased a product or service using the device. Moreover, about 75% of the survey's respondents said they were interested in making purchases or conducting other transactions through m-commerce. This was followed in March 2001 by the publication of a new study by The Strategis Group indicating that m-commerce will generate very little revenue until at least 2004. At about the same time, another study, this one by Jupiter Media Metrix, suggested that m-commerce revenues would begin to soar by the middle 2003 worldwide, possibly sooner, although only a small percentage of those revenues would come from the United States. Then, in August 2001, the market research firm eMarketer said all predictions about the future of m-commerce should be taken with a grain of salt. This was after eMarketer told its clients that m-commerce would generate between $700 million and $27 billion in 2004. (The Strategis Group pegged m-commerce revenues at just over $5 billion in 2004.)

Unbiased Wisdom

Corporations pay technology analysts an estimated $15 billion a year for what *Darwin* magazine calls their "unbiased wisdom." As *Darwin* put it, "For harried executives beset by vendor hype, this measured counsel is worth the millions paid annually for subscription services and more customized advice." The numbers, particularly if they are even borderline outrageous, also help prime venture capitalists with enough data to support their decisions to create new companies and new products or services. Some old-time VCs claim they don't take market research very seriously, but their investments hype them mercilessly. The entire process is often enhanced by business executives and engineers who, like journalists, throw in a few numbers or a positive analysis attributable to an "independent analyst" when they contribute bylined articles to magazines.

The financial community usually cuts it a little closer with its market analysis. As reported by MbusinessDaily.com in July 2001: "Shares of wireless companies rose Monday after a pair of influential analysts issued research reports suggesting that the troubled sector, which has been sinking since last fall, might have hit bottom and is on the brink of recovery. Merrill Lynch analyst Steven Milunovich upgraded his recommendation for the sector to equal weight from underweight. 'Our analysts are seeing more modest estimate revisions and inventories back to normal levels by the end of the summer,' he wrote in his report."

Gallium-arsenide integrated circuits, or GaAs (pronounced "gas"), ICs are a good example of what can happen when market researchers get hold of a new or emerging technology. GaAs ICs have certain qualities that lend themselves to a number of important applications, such as wireless communications and military hardware. In the early 1980s, as the first dramatic research for GaAs large-scale integration and complex microwave IC development was disclosed, market research organizations began to find a market for GaAs IC studies and projected sales of these devices in the multibillion-dollar range by 1990.

As it turned out, the projections were much too high. High enough that by 1985, nearly 50 companies had built GaAs IC manufacturing facilities. This led to another round of studies, which also sold well, predicting vast overcapacity of GaAs IC manufacturing. Estimates put GaAs IC sales in the $80 million to $150 million range, but a market background paper published by TriQuint Semiconductor (a leading GaAs IC vendor) in 1987 placed actual standard GaAs component sales at "probably no more than $10 million."

Curiously, few in the industry were ready to blame the market research community. Where there was true demand for GaAs ICs, most of it—perhaps 80% to 90%—was captive. In other words, most of the GaAs ICs being manufactured were being used in products produced by the same companies that made the GaAs ICs. There were simply too many merchant suppliers and not enough legitimate outside customers to make GaAs ICs a viable business, at least not in the mid-1980s.

Trade associations are also a major source of market information. Many of them have expanded their research activities, adding in-depth interpretations of industry trends and economic data to the traditional surveys they conduct themselves while commissioning additional studies by independent market research groups.

Whether they believe the data or not, special interest groups don't hesitate to use market research if it advances their cause. In 1986, the Electronic Industries Association's (EIA) Microwave Tube Division used charts and graphs from a variety of sources—some of them unnamed—to support a study that indicated a steady decline in microwave tube R&D. The following year, the Institute of Electrical and Electronics Engineers' (IEEE)

Microwave Theory and Techniques Society's Committee to Promote National Microwave Standards published market-related charts and tables, including several developed by the U.S. Commerce Department, to make a case for the declining state of microwave metrology in the United States. That same year, a report by the Pentagon's Defense Science Task Force recommending the establishment of a consortium of U.S. semiconductor producers was loaded with market statistics, all aimed at supporting the board's initiative.

With all the research that high-tech companies and other organizations produce and purchase, the federal government remains the primary source of market data. And even that isn't enough to satisfy industry needs. Remember the Strategic Defense Initiative (SDI)? More popularly known as "Star Wars," it was a massive federal government program aimed at using advanced technology to reduce or remove the threat of a nuclear attack on the United States. In 1986, Business Communications Co. created a great deal of excitement within the military establishment with a study titled *The Strategic Defense Initiative: Business Opportunities and Technological Potential*. The study concluded that the potential for commercial spinoffs in more than 18 major technologies would prove "staggering, perhaps providing sales from $5 trillion to $20 trillion." But when BCC tried to sell a copy of its $1,750 report to U.S. Air Force Col. James Ball, who was then director of the SDI Technology Applications Office and responsible for transferring SDI-sponsored technology to private industry, Ball declined. Asked about efforts to forecast the potential for SDI technology in commercial applications, Ball said at the time, "I don't think it's a productive exercise."

Even author John Rhea ended his 1988 book, *SDI—What Could Happen (8 Possible Star Wars Scenarios)*, on a self-deprecating note with a reference to a Huck Finn commentary on *The Adventures of Tom Sawyer*. It is, said Huck, "mostly a true book, with some stretchers."

How about a study comparing the out-year forecasts of leading high-tech analysts with actual sales today? The personal digital assistant (PDA) is a good test example. In 1993,

John Sculley, then president of Apple Computer, quoted the projected size of the handheld computer market at $3 trillion. This begs the question: Did Apple start up its Newton Messagepad development based on this market projection, or did analysts start covering this market segment because it seemed like a good opportunity to sell a lot of market studies?

TRUE STORY

In the summer of 1980, I was the editor and associate publisher of a now defunct magazine then published by Billboard Publications. Called *Merchandising*, it focused on the consumer electronics industry, but it also kept pretty good track of small and large appliances because most retailers who sold consumer electronics also displayed and sold hair dryers, food mixers, dishwashers, dryers, microwave ovens, and other appliances. At least, they did at the time.

We wrote for the entire industry, including manufacturers, but our audience was mainly retailers. And we did a lot of market research, which we gave away simply by publishing the results. In fact, our research was quoted in so many other business publications that we created a promotion piece to hype what we perceived to be our growing status as an industry voice.

This was reenforced by a call I received from the marketing director of *Better Homes and Gardens* magazine, who suggested that we meet to discuss something of potentially mutual interest. Sounded interesting. So, we did lunch.

It seems that *BH&G*'s editors had become convinced that women, including a large percentage of *BH&G*'s readers, actually bought their own TV sets, stereo systems, and other consumer electronic products. They made these purchase decisions pretty much on their own and, most of the time, used their own money to pay for them. With that piece of market intelligence, *BH&G* decided that it would survey 2,500 of its readers to "prove" to potential advertisers that this was true. Up to this point, *BH&G* wasn't getting any advertising dollars out of this market category. In fact, it wasn't even pursuing it.

The survey was essential. *BH&G*, and other magazines owned by its parent company, Meredith Corp., as a matter of policy, didn't make a move without researching its readers first. *BH&G* hoped to show advertisers that it made a lot of sense for them to spend a chunk of their ad budgets in *BH&G*.

But they didn't know much about the marketplace. What are the industry's new product introduction schedules, and who were the lead players? And could they get a look at copies of our survey questionnaires as a jumping-off point for developing their own questionnaires? Could we work something out? We did and it turned out to be a much more interesting exercise for *BH&G* than for us.

The *BH&G* ad sales and marketing team, at least three of them, armed with a brand new sales presentation loaded with can't-miss data out of its reader survey, made its first call on RCA Consumer Electronics in Indianapolis. The RCA people listened quietly and patiently to the entire pitch. And then they jumped all over the *BH&G* team.

Why should RCA put any money into a home decorating magazine, they asked, that never shows a TV set in a kitchen? Or in a living room? People do have TV sets in their kitchens. Not just in their dens and bedrooms. Everyone knows this. Why doesn't *BH&G*?

Of course, RCA knew the answer, and so did the *BH&G* people. The magazine's design staff simply wouldn't allow that ugly box—a TV set—to mess up their editorial picture layouts. The lines, the flow, the ambience of a carefully designed kitchen or living room simply wouldn't allow for such a thing. Forget the reality, if it messes up the look of the room—and it usually did according to *BH&G* designers/decorators and page layout staff—it was out.

RCA wasn't going to play *BH&G*'s game. As RCA made clear to the *BH&G* people, KITCHENS HAVE TV SETS. Either put them where they belong, RCA said, or it had no interest in advertising in this multimillion circulation magazine.

With that information in hand, the slightly stunned and bowed *BH&G* people trudged back to New York to inform their ad director and publisher that if they expected to get any ad money out of TV manufacturers, they would have to go back to the drawing boards. And they did.

Ready for My Closeup

There is something in the movie and television world known as product placement that is a much-sought-after opportunity by consumer product manufacturers. With literally millions of people viewing first-run movies throughout the world and then in TV reruns and home video, they have become a highly effective and relatively cheap way to boost consumer awareness of a new product.

Car manufacturers and fashion designers have been playing this game for years and they frequently get screen credits for their "contribution" to the film. Mercedes-Benz's new SUV made its first public appearance in *Jurassic Park II*. Victoria's Secret models were featured on the TV sitcom "Spin City" in a story involving the show's characters trying to get tickets to the annual Victoria's Secret Fashion Show.

E.T. probably helped sell a lot of Reese's Pieces. And Frank Sinatra always made sure that his favorite New York restaurant, Jilly's, made an appearance in at least one scene in any movie he could work it into. (Haven't seen a "Cigarettes provided by Phillip Morris" in a movie credit yet, but I may have simply missed it.) And how could you miss James Bond's highly customized Aston Martin, or his movie-to-movie bantering with M, the head of British Secret service, about his favorite sidearm, a Beretta?

High-tech products are now starring in major motion pictures and TV shows with increasing frequency. And it's not very subtle. Remember Tom Cruise holding his cellular phone with the brightly lit Motorola logo up to the camera in the middle of a high-speed chase in *Mission Impossible 2*?

Good timing and planning also helps. Paramount Pictures released its action flick, *Tomb Raider*, starring cyber-heroine Lara Croft (played by Oscar-winning actress Angelina Jolie), just as Ericsson was ramping up deliveries of its wireless Bluetooth headset, a new cordless Webscreen, a stylish new hip-mounted communicator, and a range of new high-tech wireless accessories. The Webscreen H610, which is a real Ericsson product, according to the heavy-handed copy "is the perfect rugged traveling companion for Lara as she encounters extreme conditions at every turn."

Ericsson phones also played a prominent role in the 1997 James Bond film, *Tomorrow Never Dies*, in which 007 used an Ericsson concept phone the company said in press releases "captured people's imagination about the future." Click to

Ericsson's "Tomb Raider" Web page and you will find a picture of the Bluetooth headset, along with the caption, "Whenever Lara is in trouble, she's never in a mess. That's because she uses a Bluetooth headset. It connects with your phone wirelessly, so you can call, answer and talk as you move around—without any cables to get in the way."

Val Kilmer could never have pulled off half of his tricks in Paramount Pictures' 1997 action film, *The Saint*, without Nokia's clamshell-style 9000 Communicator. So much so that the Nokia device deserved a better screen credit. In the film, the Kilmer character continuously relies on the phone and its computing features to get out of tight situations and to calculate his next move. Heikki Norta, general manager of market services for Nokia Mobile Phones in Europe and Africa, provided the early hype. "It makes a real statement about Nokia's products when a movie like 'The Saint,' which features cutting-edge technology and uses so many sophisticated devices, has selected the Nokia 9000 Communicator from a vast array of existing or potential products," she said. To get even more mileage out of the exposure, an original *The Saint* Internet competition, involving Volvo as well as Nokia, ran worldwide. One of the prizes was a Nokia 9000 with $50,000 worth of free airtime. Nokia products were also used in *Bridget Jones's Diary*.

Aikido specialist Steven Seagal would never have been able to save the world from high-tech terrorists in *Under Siege* without the aid of Apple Computer's ill-fated Newton electronic organizer. Tight closeups of the Newton unit faxing a distress message from the fast-moving train to the Seagal character's friend were very effective, if grossly overdone.

On TV, there was little mistaking Apple Computer's colorful and funky-shaped iMac desktop PCs on the now canceled San Francisco cop show "Nash Bridges." More recently, Apple got another huge plug when actor Ben Stiller, playing a spectacularly stupid male model, tries to break open an Apple iMac in the movie *Zoolander* when his character is told the information he wants is "in the computer."

The reality TV series, "Survivor," has prominently integrated products in its show. As Producer Mark Burnett told *Esquire* magazine, "My shows create an interest and people will look at them, but the endgame here is selling products in stores—a car, deodorant, running shoes. It's the future of television." In the show's second season, "Survivor: The Australian Outback," players competed for several highly visible prizes, from a Pontiac Aztek to a VISA-sponsored online shopping spree.

In September 2001, ABC TV was scheduled to debut "The Runner," another reality-based show in which the central figure tries to cross the country undetected while completing a series of tasks for a $1 million prize. One scenario would have the "runner" drop into a Starbucks for a decaf latte or (the high-tech angle) pull out his Nokia cellphone to check his e-mail.

In almost none of these cases does the manufacturer pay to place its products in the film. But it can lead to some costly cross-marketing arrangements. Early in 2001, for example, Nokia promoted Sony Pictures remake of the 1970's hit TV series, "Charlie's Angels." Picking up on the same theme used in the original series, the angels never see their boss, Charlie. He calls them to discuss their investigation. Same thing in the remake, only the angels conspicuously use Nokia phones to talk to Charlie. Nokia's part of the deal, besides supplying the phones for the movie, was to create and sponsor in-store promotions and TV ads to help promote the movie.

How far can you take this?

While books have long been the jumping-off point for movie scripts, the newest grist for the movie mill is much more high-tech—videogames. That's how films like *Tomb Raider* and *Final Fantasy* made it to the big screen; they started as very popular games. *Mortal Kombat*, released in 1995, was another successful game-to-movie. An Internet game designed to promote Steven Spielberg's sci-fi epic *A.I.* (as in artificial intelligence) was so popular that its creators decided to continue it through the summer of 2001, while the movie was still playing strong in theaters across the country. Designed by Microsoft for Warner Bros., the *A.I.* game features an imaginary future society similar to the one portrayed in the movie. A few other games, such as Super Mario Brothers (1993) and Wing Commander (1999), didn't do very well. Street Fighter (1994) generated more than $100 million, mostly overseas. By mid-2001, the rights to at least eight videogames had been acquired by movie studios.

One of the most aggressive game/movie efforts was for *Swordfish*, the splashy, heavy-on-special effects Warner Bros. movie, starring John Travolta. The film recorded a huge boost in traffic in the week following the launch of its online sweepstakes, which included a game associated with the movie. Players can go offline or online for a scavenger hunt to find passwords for the game. The passwords allow the Web site visitors access to areas of the site where they can view movie stills, animated stunts, and special-effects scenes.

AOL Instant Messaging even got into the act when Warner set up an AOL account under the name Gabriel Shear, the name of the spy played by Travolta in the movie, through which consumers can chat with the character and receive information about the movie. This worked very well for Warner: Something like five messages a second were received in the few weeks following the movie's release. Not to miss any portable hit, the studio also was beaming passwords via wireless infrared links to PDAs from telephone-kiosk posters in New York.

The next step? With the media business tight and likely to get tighter, TV viewers will be seeing more "contributions" from companies that are willing to try just about any innovative marketing scheme to reach consumers who are becoming more resistant to traditional methods of promoting products. Increasingly, this will be done with digital technology. Most likely, it will use a technology developed by Princeton Video Image.

PVI's technology enables television stations to electronically sneak an advertiser's logo, for example, into the background of a program.

Using PVI's system, baseball viewers can see a logo for a soft drink on the backstop behind home plate during the first few innings of the game and a different logo during the rest of the game. "The Early Show" on CBS TV superimposes its logo just about anywhere by using PVI's technology, including PVI's digital technology. PVI has also provided virtual signage during "The NFL Today" pre-game show on CBS for the first time in a studio sports program, inserting sponsored logos and various program graphics into the pre-game broadcast. PVI has also provided virtual ads for several local advertisers during NFL games. (Roy Rosser, one of the founders of PVI, even had this idea that you could slip all advertising into the show itself without ever going to a commercial break.)

PVI has also signed on to run ads on the electronically displayed yellow first-down line during NFL games. Okay, why not run news headlines and the closing stock market prices from the previous Friday on the same yellow first-down marker during NFL games, maybe with a "Courtesy of Charles Schwab" tag line?

Trade Shows: Walking the Walk

Can there possibly be any sector of the global economy with more trade shows and conferences than technology, particularly wireless and the Internet? There are, on average, more than two computer/communications/Internet-related shows every week in the United States and at least that many somewhere else in the world. These events have always been, and continue to be, a major part of promoting high-tech products and services, including those that aren't quite ready for prime time.

Bluetooth, which can boast as many as six dedicated conferences or full-blown trade shows a week in the United States in 2001 and almost as many in Europe, is a pretty good example. And that doesn't include all of the panel and workshop sessions and exhibit space focusing on Bluetooth at more broad-based meetings, such as COMDEX and the massive International Consumer Electronics Show. Both are held in the Las Vegas Convention Center because that's the only place big enough to hold them.

Trade shows are an excellent way for publishers and trade associations to generate a tremendous amount of revenue and profit, a lot more than they could from magazine advertising or membership fees. They provide a forum to conduct business with a lot of people in one place at one time. A popular Internet magazine, for example, might produce a 20% profit, whereas a trade show sponsored by the magazine can generate 50%

profit. If not, the show was probably mismanaged, or it shouldn't have been held in the first place.

Trade shows have done well in all measurable indexes, such as net square footage of exhibit space. However, attendance growth overall was at its lowest in the fourth quarter of 2000 since 1998, increasing at a rate of only 1.9%, according to *Tradeshow Week's* Quarterly Report of Tradeshow Statistics. And after three years of substantial growth, computer and electronics exhibitions held during 1999 reported almost no increase in net square feet and exhibiting companies.

Although attendance figures were up slightly the previous year, overall growth rates were unimpressive, according to *Tradeshow Week's* Eighth Annual Computer & Electronics Show Report. Computer and electronics shows increased 0.2% in both net square feet and exhibiting companies and 3.1% in professional attendance. (Trade show sponsors put out some very slick brochures on their shows, usually with pie charts showing who attends and how many. If you really want to know the strength of a show, get the actual attendance figure, not registrations. And if you really want to be pushy, ask the trade show manager how many of the attendees are not exhibitors—that is, the number of people not actually manning their company's booths.)

Not surprisingly, about 250 meetings and conventions were canceled in Las Vegas in September and October 2001, most of them following the September 11 terrorist attacks on New York and the Pentagon. Several high-tech conferences were either canceled or delayed. Still, with so many trade shows to choose from and a faltering economy, the entire concept of meeting and greeting competitors and customers in one place has come into question, particularly among high-tech companies.

Curiously, the technical programs (conferences, workshops, panels) at technical symposiums have become stronger as the economy continued to slip, mainly because companies sent their strongest technical people to key meetings to talk about what their company can do. They view this as a relatively cheap, but effective, solution to the traditional alternative, which is making as much noise as possible on the exhibit floor. In fact, the exhibits at most trade shows—the element of these shows that generates the most revenue—are getting weaker, with fewer companies attending fewer shows and sending fewer people to staff their booths, which are getting smaller. And they're spending less on entertainment at trade shows.

Sponsors have developed a number of techniques to maintain or grow their shows, usually by keeping up with, or even trying to stay ahead of, industry trends. The International Consumer Electronics Show was quick to recognize the importance of mobile communications and created a special section on the show floor for cellular phones, pagers, and other wireless vendors just as "wireless" was beginning to become another "next big thing," pulling more retail buyers to the show floor. The show's sponsor also developed a new series of workshops to cover mobile communications. The CES did the same thing when Bluetooth began to attract a lot of industry attention by creating a special section for exhibitors, some of them first-time CES attendees, just for Bluetooth products.

INFOCOMM International had the same idea when it included several specialized sections at its show, allowing greater exposure to smaller companies. A separate e-commerce section at the 1999 Minneapolis Strictly Business Computer Expo resulted in a 25% increase in exhibiting companies. Aggressive advertising helped the Fall Internet World nearly double its exhibiting companies and attendance.

Indeed, hype helps. It usually starts with calls to industry editors to set up interviews with company executives at the show and to invite editors to company-sponsored press conferences and receptions. It's not unusual for an editor from an important industry magazine to receive 30 or more calls or written invitations to interview an executive or attend a company function during a trade show, usually to talk about or hear about a "unique" new product or service.

Meanwhile, the trade show industry is still going strong, with an overall yearly attendance increase of 7.4%, a 9.3% annual jump in exhibit space, and budgets that have expanded an average of 18.7% in 2000 and 2001, according to *EXPO* magazine, whose readers are producing more shows now than they did in 1999.

Getting Technical

Unfortunately, there are too many lost opportunities for trade show attendees who find themselves sitting through technical presentations that too often amount to long commercials on products or services of the presenter's company. Trade show sponsors are usually so happy to line up "good" speakers for their workshops and seminars that they simply refuse to instill any discipline in the people they recruit, particularly since they usually don't pay them or pay any of their expenses.

Are there too many trade shows? Definitely, according to the people who usually attend them. Which is why some companies readily volunteer their key executives as panelists and even keynote speakers, which gives their company wide exposure and is a lot cheaper than paying the often exorbitant fees required for them to exhibit at these shows.

TRUE STORY

I had just turned the corner of a long aisle of exhibitors heading for the Penton Media booth, the sponsor of this trade show—the Wireless/Portable Symposium & Exhibition. The show was held, as it had been since it's inception, at the Santa Clara Convention Center in the heart of Silicon Valley.

Like most large trade and business magazine publishers, Penton also sponsors trade shows and seminars, usually related to the industries their magazines cover. As the editor of Penton's *Wireless Systems Design* magazine, I served (more or less) as a technical adviser to the show—mainly suggesting keynote speaker candidates and workshop topics and potential presenters, for example. In addition, as the editor of one of the company's magazines, I was expected to serve as a "front" for the show, introducing speakers at technical sessions.

As I approached the Penton booth, I noticed Jeff, an outside contractor Penton hired to handle the show's logistics, waving at me frantically.

"You just missed them," he said.

"Who?"

"The guys from Army Intelligence."

"Excuse me?"

"Yeah, there were two guys here about 15 or 20 minutes ago. Identified themselves as U.S. Army Intelligence agents. They said they wanted to talk to you."

"They want to talk to *me*?"

"That's right."

"They asked for me by name?"

"Yes."

"What did you tell them?"

"I told them that I would try to track you down and see if you would meet with them at the trade show office at 3 p.m."

I looked at my watch. It was coming up on 1:30. I had some time to kill, but that's okay. I was walking the show anyway, talking to exhibitors, trying to get updated on some industry issues, what some of these companies were going to be doing in the next several months. And, of course, most important to them, since I was the editor of an industry magazine with a pretty healthy circulation, checking out their new products. Publishers love it when editors talk to potential advertisers. If they had their way, that's all editors would do.

Jeff asked if I was going to meet with them.

"Of course."

I started down the aisle, looking ahead, trying to figure out where I wanted to make my next booth stop. I got to the end of the aisle, turned right and continued walking, crossing over two or three numbered aisles, when I noticed a tall, blond guy in a blue suit and rep tie, probably in his mid-30s, approaching. He moved directly into my path and reached into his jacket pocket. Since we had never met, I can only assume that he read my name on my show badge. A good trick from 20 to 30 feet away.

"Mr. Schneiderman, I'm Special Agent Bishop, U.S. Army Intelligence, out of the Presidio (the big Army installation at the south end of the Golden Gate Bridge, about 40 miles up the road from Silicon Valley). He flashed his ID, including a badge. He even had a business card, which he gave me.

"Can we take a walk?," he said.

This was great. Just like in the movies. As we started up an aisle, Special Agent Bishop's partner pulled up along the other side of me, introduced himself, showed his ID, and handed me his card. No indication of their military rank, but that's the way it works with these guys.

Bishop launched into his speech. God and country. Started talking about how important it is to protect our nation's secrets from certain "foreign nationals." Especially advanced technology. He said that I was obviously very aware of this issue and must be sensitive to it in my position. I didn't respond. I figured this was going somewhere, so I just kept listening.

Another minute or so of politics and the potential dangers we face as a country and then Bishop and his partner began to focus their pitch. They wanted me to supply them with the names of "foreign nationals" attending the show, including those who worked for American companies, which they assumed (accurately) I could access. Better yet, how about the actual registration forms that these people had to fill out to get into the show? The applications would have their employers names and, by extension, would indicate their specific areas of technical interest and other personal data that might prove useful.

What were they going to do with this information? Turns out that this Presideo-based crew was monitoring foreign interest in U.S. technology in Silicon Valley and was building a database of names and other information. At some point, they would analyze the data and determine, among other things, what people from what countries, working for what companies, were interested in what technologies.

"Follow me," I said.

Fortunately, my boss, the publisher of my magazine, who also served as the general manager of the show, was in the Penton booth. I waved to him to join us. The four of us went off into a corner and after the introductions, I invited the agents to repeat their request. They did, but before my boss could respond, Special Agent Bishop said that they would send us a letter formalizing their request for the information they were seeking, probably within the week.

Sounds good, my boss said, adding that we would respond to the letter in a timely fashion. They thanked us for our time and said they would appreciate our cooperation "on this matter." And they left.

Jeff showed up only minutes later.

"Did you meet with those guys?" he said.

"Yes, I did, Jeff."

"What did they want?"

"I can't tell you."

"You're kidding."

"Well, I could tell you, but then I'd have to kill you."

"No, I'm serious," he said.

I leaned in close to Jeff, put on my best 007 expression and said, "So am I."

We never heard from anyone in Army Intelligence. Never received a letter. Either they just forgot about us, or they got the information without our help.

But there is one question that the few people familiar with this event could never clear up, including me. Why did they ask for me? The only reason I could think of, and it's kind of weak, is that I was the only member of the Penton Media staff involved in the show in any way with military service. U.S. Air Force, Strategic Air Command (SAC), four years, and I had a high security clearance. Did they run all of our names and mine was the only one that blinked on their computer screen? Was I the most likely, then, to be sympathetic to their request for information?

Don't know. And it's too late to ask. The Presidio was closed down shortly after our meeting.

Have I Got an Article for You

One of the things that many technology companies are very good at is placing homegrown articles in industry magazines. They're usually written by an engineer or marketing executive—often with professional editorial help. Some are farmed out to a PR firm or freelance writer who specializes in technical writing or editing.

The results can be very effective.

In one year, in the mid-1990s, Texas Instruments, with some very aggressive help from one of its Houston-based PR agencies, placed nearly 250 articles in industry magazines. Obviously, you have to have a very healthy budget for this, but it's still a lot cheaper than advertising, especially if you count the pages at the end of the year. Hewlett-Packard and its spinoff instrumentation group, Agilent Systems, are also very good at this process. At one time, Agilent's PR staff put together a list of more than 200 article ideas but backed off when someone figured out what it was going to cost in freelance fees to generate all of these features. (At least $700,000 is a good round number guess).

Many high-tech industry magazines, including some of the most respected publications in their industry, use a combination of staff-written and contributed articles. Of course, the articles are bylined by the "author," even if the actual or final writing is done by someone else. One of the things an editor has to expect and accept is that the article (at best) will promote a technology that the author and his or her company is developing and promoting, with at least a brief mention somewhere in the article of the company's contribution to the field, including a product or service. At its worst, an entire article can turn out to be a commercial for the contributing company's new process or product.

The Press Release

Of course, press or news releases have always been a staple of high-tech PR. One of the more aggressive approaches currently is the prerelease, a news release about the real release that's coming. A company or trade association sends out a release a week or so in advance of the actual release, not so much to get advance coverage (although this happens, particularly in publications with sharp, knowledgeable, and very aggressive editors and reporters who can ferret out additional details), but to help promote coverage of the actual announcement to follow.

As Yogi Berra would say, it's *deja vu* all over again.

Good Examples, Good News

S ome products and services are destined for success. Hype or no hype, they're going to make it. For software-defined radios, the news is just getting out. Artificial intelligence, or AI, on the other hand, has been kicking around for nearly half a century. Despite the poorly reviewed Steven Spielberg movie, A.I., about a very lifelike robotic boy who is programmed to love the people who adopt him, AI survives and is finally beginning to flourish in some applications, even if they're hidden and almost no one knows about them or understands the technology. Smart cards are old news waiting to make it big with an upgraded technology—embedded chips with the capacity to store huge amounts of personal data, as well as the ability to transmit that data through the Internet and other global networks.

Entertainment may be the next high ground for high-tech. Electronic games are huge right now, even supplanting books as the jumping-off point for several movies. Wireless porn may be next. As Michael J. Wolf, a senior partner of the Media and Enter-

tainment Group at Booz-Allen & Hamilton, a management consultancy, wrote in his 1999 book, The Entertainment Economy–How Mega-Media Forces Are Transforming Our Lives, on how the global economy will be defined by hits and blockbusters: "As one consumer company after another joined the stampede to the Internet, they realized that they had to fill those Web pages with things that would inform, amuse, and most of all, entertain masses of people. Locally, globally, internationally, we are living in an entertainment economy."

The next big development is mobile games . . . fun on-the-fly. Titles are already being released that represent an entire range of current mobile gaming technologies, including Short Messaging Services (SMS), Wireless Application Protocols (WAP), Java, and Qualcomm's BREW.

In fact, there are a number of examples of technologies that will very likely generate truly big numbers in the marketplace—technologies that will rise above the hype.

Over-the-Air Cellular Phone Repair

Imagine this conversation with your cellular phone service provider:

"Hello, I'm calling with a question. But not on my cellphone, because it doesn't work."

"Is it the RoboTalk Model 37X/39?"

"Yes, it is. And that's why I'm calling."

"Okay," the carrier guys says, "the story is that we discovered that it has a software flaw. It needs a fix. We were going to send you a letter about the problem, but since you called, we can take care of it now."

"You mean I have to bring it in today? I won't have my cellphone for a week or two, right?"

"No, we'll take care of it from here. Just leave the phone on and we'll take care of it now."

"Excuse me?"

Enter software-defined radio, or SDR, technology. It's not quite available on any commercial scale yet, but it will be soon. And probably just in time.

Remember the spate of cellphone recalls in the summer of 2001? Nokia created a huge headache in the CDMA digital cellular world when it discovered that its handsets were not compatible with next-generation cdma2000 1X cellular networks. Cellphone subscribers on CDMA networks didn't know what was going on other than the fact that their phones wouldn't connect. Then, Sony announced the recall of 1.1 million cellphones, also because software flaws made them incompatible with the network. Japan's biggest wireless operator, NTT DoCoMo, was next, announcing that it would repair about 100,000 of its Matsushita Communications-produced cellphones when they couldn't receive incoming calls at certain locations. A few days later, Japan's second largest wireless carrier, KDDI, said that it would offer free software upgrades to fix the more than 52,000 digital cdmaOne phones that lost access to service when KDDI attempted to upgrade its equipment for a new high-speed data service scheduled to go online beginning in the fall.

Nokia described the problem as a simple "bug fixing." Sony had to take a $95 million charge in its first fiscal quarter to pay its recall costs. But they all had a big PR problem because all of these phones had to be returned to the shop for service, which means that a lot of people were without cellphone service for a while.

SDRs could eliminate most of these problems by reconfiguring—in other words, fixing or upgrading the software—over the air and without having to install new hardware or software. Over-the-air software downloading is one of the areas that network and service providers are developing to essentially eliminate the need to physically return wireless phones to the carrier for service. This is an eminently hypeable feature and can save them a ton of money. Which means that wireless service subscribers will be hearing a lot more about it—in time.

SDR is well suited to the task. It can change a radio's bandwidth, modulation, and waveforms with wirelessly transmitted software commands.

The U.S. Air Force started seriously playing around with SDR in 1989 under a program called the Tactical Anti-Jam

Programmable Signal Processor (TAJPSP). The program captured the attention of the other U.S. military services and quickly developed into a tri-service project called SPEAKeasy. The idea was to develop a modular, reprogrammable and open (meaning nonproprietary) system and to create a generic software architecture to facilitate the programming of additional waveforms. With its potential to provide communications between different types of radios in use at any time by any of the military services (even foreign military services in some instances)—as well as its ability to accept upgrades and software fixes over the air—SDR was kicked upstairs to Defense Department-level status and has since developed into a baseline architecture that is now the jumping-off point for several SDR systems in development today, most of them for commercial and consumer use.

SDR got a big break in December 2000 when the Federal Communications Commission (FCC) issued what it calls a notice of proposed rulemaking to speed the adoption of SDR technology in the United States. The commission's proposal would permit manufacturers to make, for the first time, certain changes in power, frequency, and modulation without refiling authorizations with the FCC to operate with each change. It also proposed the use of electronic labeling so that the radio won't have to be returned to the manufacturer for relabeling, effectively allowing software modifications in the field.

SDR still isn't ready for prime time. But because of its ability to download upgrades and fixes and even potentially new applications, most analysts expect SDR to begin to find its way into next-generation cellular phones. Projections by selected "industry experts" interviewed by The SDR Forum, the lead organization for promoting the technology, is for 134 million to 201 million SDR-based devices to be in the market by 2005.

Some U.S. chip houses have begun promoting multistandard ICs as a step toward configurable wireless communications, or chips that can detect any digital wireless transmission standard and reconfigure it on-the-fly. Others are developing a totally new class of reconfigurable digital ICs that will be embedded directly into cellular handsets.

International interest in SDR also is strong. The SDR Forum has held several workshops for Japanese and European telecommunications regulators, and Japan's Ministry for Communications is expected to write its own set of regulations for the certification of SDR equipment in Japan.

Expectations for SDR are high. SDR offers wireless radio manufacturers an opportunity to prolong the life of their products, cut costly inventories, and promote a new and highly marketable selling feature. With few exceptions, this means no more losing the use of the phone if it has to be returned to the shop.

Get Smart (Cards)

One of the quietest, yet most pervasive, technology developments currently underway is smart cards, those wallet-size plastic cards that store information on either a magnetic strip or an embedded microchip. Smart cards work like prepaid cards but have intelligence built into them, enabling them to be used for a variety of functions, not just phone calls.

You may think you're already familiar with these, but new versions are being developed that should solve a few lingering and annoying technical problems. Meanwhile, credit card companies, retailers, banks, and other financial institutions are heavily promoting their use for even the simplest transactions, including those conducted over cellular phones and wireless-enabled personal digital assistants (PDAs).

Unlike the case in Europe, where smart cards are used almost everywhere, including almost every digital cellphone, the use of these cards in the United States has pretty much been limited to older, much less secure magnetic-strip credit cards. In fact, until recently, U.S. sales of smart cards represented barely more than 2% of the industry's global total, compared to 60% in Europe. This is going to change, and soon. American Express, VISA, and MasterCard have issued millions of these cards, and they're just getting started.

Smart cards aren't new. But with the intelligence that can now be embedded in a tiny chip embossed on the card (your credit status and medical history, for example), they're getting a lot smarter.

The Bell System started it all, introducing its so-called post-paid calling card in 1939. Made of cardboard and issued annually to mostly business travelers to make calls and pay for them later, the cards required an operator to verify the identity of the caller. It wasn't until 1980 that phone company customers could complete calls without operator intervention. That's when AT&T introduced its Universal Card, combining a post-paid phone card with a typical credit card. Prepaid cards, in which customers pay in advance for a certain number of calls or for a specific amount of time, were introduced in Italy in 1976, mainly to combat pay phone vandalism. Phone companies also liked them because they reduced the cost of coin collection and service calls.

Chicago-based Ameritech was the first major American telecom carrier to introduce prepaid calling cards in the United States. Another carrier, US West, introduced smart cards for pay phones in 1994, but their growth has been hindered primarily by the need to standardize the cards so they're all compatible and tie them into the development of point-of-sale terminals—enabling consumers to use any of these new cards at any retail outlet.

Surprisingly, one of the industry's biggest problems is increasing consumer awareness. The U.S.-based Telecommunications Industry Association says smart cards represent one of the fastest-growing segments of the telecommunications market. But with the wireless Web and electronic and mobile commerce expected to grow dramatically, as well as the need to provide other new services requiring high levels of security (online banking, stock trading, even gambling), even the most risk-averse U.S. financial institutions are beginning to take them more seriously. MasterCard International, which has already sold more than 30 million smart cards in Japan, Europe, and Latin America, is following the lead of VISA and American Express with its own smart card to handle secure online purchases made through its 28,000-member banks in the United States.

A New Meaning to Calling Cards

It wasn't until the Global System for Mobile Communications (GSM) was approved as the technical standard for digital cellular throughout Europe that chip-based smart cards gained any prominence. Subscriber identity modules, or SIM cards, were developed so they could be slipped into slots specifically designed for them in GSM-technology based cellular phones. Each of these chip-based cards holds secure subscription data and applications for GSM wireless services. They enable GSM cardholders to use any GSM-based phone, not just their own, with the calling charges going to the owner of the card.

More than 100 SIM applications have been developed by GSM service providers around the world, including automated mobile banking and mobile trading services, location-sensitive information, and roaming services.

Gemplus International SA, which claims more than 40% marketshare for smart cards worldwide and says it has shipped more than 200 million SIM cards, has developed with Qualcomm, Inc., an interoperable CDMA/GSM SIM card and compatible handset capable of handling both the GSM and Qualcomm-developed digital CDMA transmission technology. CDMA subscribers traveling to countries using different networks, such as GSM, can remove the SIM and plug it into another handset to gain immediate access to the new network.

One of the more recent concerns in the smart-card community is security. Companies like America Express, MasterCard, and VISA have formed a new cross-industry group, the Mobile Payment Forum, to develop standards for secure mobile payments. Issues at the top of the forum's agenda include interoperability, encryption, and cardholder authentication. Industry leaders have also begun to collaborate on a position paper on the advantages of smart-card technology in personal identification systems. (Delta Air Lines began testing a smart-card system early in 2002 at London's Gatwick Airport, with the aim of increasing airline security while moving passengers more quickly to their scheduled flights.) Mobile commerce requires security, but its biggest role may turn out to be in driving the development of multiapplication cards and new products. Several companies have announced or are developing a new generation of smart-card microcontrollers or other types of chips that are optimized for multiple applications in mobile communications. They also support public key infrastructure (PKI) cryptography to ensure authentic and private communications over the Internet, in either wired or wireless applications.

The telecom industry has already started testing high-end GSM Java cards and Universal IC cards (compatible with today's SIM cards and GSM networks) for next-generation portable phones. As GSM developments advance, they're expected to rely more heavily on SIM cards for operational functions of the network for system authentication, roaming, and service information.

Now that the smart-card industry is well on its way to solving most of its technical problems and has virtually all the major financial institutions onboard, it is focusing on pitching its technology to the masses in the United States. The Smart Card Industry Association and the Smart Card Forum merged during 2000 into an aggressive single industry voice called the Smart Card Alliance, with a new network security initiative for the American market.

Two big issues are still on the industry's plate. One is infrastructure; that is, how to build and deploy enough card-readers to keep up with the expected demand, and training people to use them. The other is privacy: selling the public on a government-sponsored—essentially a national ID—security card. The smart-card people don't openly advocate national ID cards, but they're making a good case for smart cards for secure identification.

How Smart Is Artificial Intelligence?

What's the acceptable mean time between when a technology first hits the public consciousness and when it becomes, more or less, reality? For anyone seriously interested in artificial intelligence, or AI, it's a long time.

Arthur C. Clarke's vision, expressed through HAL, the plain-speaking but powerful computer in the 1968 sci-fi movie *2001: A Space Odyssey*, got many people thinking for the first time about what computers might be able to do, even on their own. It was a little scary at first. Fewer books and articles have been published on AI in the past four or five years. One noteworthy exception was the five-page feature in *BusinessWeek* (August 7, 2000), headlined, "Thinking Machines—After years of hype and letdowns, computers are starting to acquire real factory smarts."

And in some strange form of reverse hype, the *New York Times* published a feature on the state of AI technology just as the movie *A.I.* was being introduced in theaters across the country. The *Times* didn't like the movie . . . few reviewers did. Despite Spielberg's earlier successes with such films as *Close Encounters of the Third Kind* and *E.T.: The Extraterrestrial*, the three-hour-long *A.I.* did not do well beyond its first weekend in U.S. theaters. Its "Pinocchio-yearns-to-become-a-'real-boy'-so-his-parents-will-love-him" theme turned off people who expected something else, something more, from Spielberg. It just didn't measure up among sci-fi fans. (Indeed, *A.I.* paled next to *Matrix*, the 1999 cyber-fantasy action release starring Keanu Reeves, which featured not only special effects, but some off-the-wall—literally—martial arts.)

But the *Times* piece did make the point that AI has been around since at least the 1950s when the first conferences on the subject were beginning to be held and some of the first AI labs were established. A number of those labs have disappeared, and some big corporations with an interest in AI significantly reduced their investment in this work as long ago as the mid 1980s. As Steven A. Ward, the founder and CEO of Ward Systems Group said in the *Times* article, "Some technology managers still associate artificial intelligence with the hype of that era."

How big is AI? It's hard to tell, mainly because it is usually hidden in larger programs. (BIAP Systems, for example, which specializes in developing intelligent agents and expert system technology, says it has successfully embedded AI-based software in broadband television set-top boxes, enabling the boxes to offer subscribers enhanced features without additional hardware.) This "hide the AI" aspect of the technology is called the

AI Effect, and it helps explain how technologies that have been around for years and that may actually be thriving by most standards, can get lost in the shuffle.

James Hogan, in his book *Mind Matters*, offers this explanation of the AI Effect: "AI researchers talk about a peculiar phenomenon known as the AI Effect. At the outset of a project, the goal is to entice a performance from machines in some designated area that everyone agrees would require 'intelligence' if done by a human. If the project fails, it becomes a target of derision to be pointed at by the skeptics as an example of the absurdity of the idea that AI could be possible. If it succeeds, with the process demystified and its inner workings laid bare as lines of prosaic computer code, the subject is dismissed as 'not really all that intelligent after all.' Perhaps . . . the real threat that we resist is the further demystification of ourselves. It seems to happen repeatedly that a line of AI work finds itself being diverted in such a direction that the measures that were supposed to mark its attainment are demonstrated brilliantly. Then, the resulting new knowledge typically stimulates demands for application of it and a burgeoning industry, market, and an additional facet to our way of life comes into being, which within a decade we take for granted; but by then, of course, it isn't AI."

Stottler Henke Associates, Inc., a California-based AI player, defines the AI Effect this way: "The great practical benefits of AI applications and even the existence of AI in many software products go largely unnoticed by many despite the already widespread use of AI techniques in software. This is the AI Effect. Many marketing people don't use the term 'artificial intelligence' even when their company's products rely on some AI techniques. Why not? It may be because AI was OVERSOLD (my caps) in the first giddy days of practical rule-based expert systems in the 1980s, with the peak perhaps marked by the *BusinessWeek* cover of July 9, 1984 announcing, 'Artificial Intelligence, IT'S HERE (*BW*'s caps).'"

Actually, it's here in several forms. What some still call AI is now also known as automated computing, introspective computing, or automated reasoning, depending on the application. So-called knowledge-based systems and expert systems also fall into the realm of AI. An example is the Three Corner Sat mission Casper (continuous activity scheduling, planning, execution, and replanning) software that NASA's Jet Propulsion Laboratory plans to use on some upcoming space launch. Casper uses the input from cameras on its three satellites to make real-time decisions without human intervention . . . a classic AI application. It can even create virtual characters for video war games at the U.S. Naval Postgraduate School's Modeling, Virtual Environments, and Simulation (MOVES) Institute.

The Turing Test

The earliest thinking about how science and engineering could make intelligent machines, especially intelligent computers, came shortly after World War II. Some of the earliest ideas came from Alan M. Turing, a prominent British mathematician and middle-distance runner, whose paper "On Computing Numbers," written in 1937, described a machine that, with the proper instructions and the use of punched paper tape to control its operation, would imitate any other machine. Turing's reputation was further enhanced when he suggested in a 1950 article in *Computing Machinery and Intelligence* that if a computer could successfully impersonate a human, it could be called intelligent. This became know as the Turing Test.

Turing's work with computers and advanced mathematical theories was interrupted by the war when he spent most of his time breaking the codes of the Enigma, the German cipher machine that helped Britain secretly obtain information on the location and combat capabilities of German submarines. But the buzz for what would become AI didn't really begin to develop until 1947, when Turing in a lecture declared his interest in programming computers to make machines intelligent rather than trying to build intelligent machines.

Turing's influence is hard to measure, but Brandeis University may have taken its lead from his work with its Golem Project, an attempt to build a class of self-improving robots that can design and manufacture improved versions of themselves, all autonomously. Jordan B. Pollack, a Brandeis researcher, made news in 2000 when it was disclosed that he helped create the first machine that could design and produce other machines with virtually no human assistance. Pollack then founded Thinmail to provide wireless device users with an intelligent assistant capable of translating documents into simple text and other hands-off tasks. (Researchers at the University of California at Berkeley are trying to develop programs that represent moods and other human emotional conditions.)

In 1971, Kenneth Mark Colby, a psychologist and founder and chairman of Malibu Artificial Intelligence Works, came up with a software program called Parry (for paranoia), which could imitate a paranoid schizophrenic. Colby claimed it was the only program that could pass the Turing Test.

By the 1960s, industrial robots began to appear, along with a branch of AI called "expert systems" that could map the structure of complex chemicals. Within 10 years, computers were developed that could learn from experience and analyze spoken language. Using AI-derived techniques, a computer became the world backgammon champion. By the 1980s, fuzzy logic, a technique for assigning varying weights to data, was the hot topic among computer programmers, and massive databases were being developed to help analyze complex patterns in financial markets. AI was beginning to generate a lot of editorials in business and technical publications. Books were being published explaining this new revolution and why it was important.

But the big news at the time was the venture capital that was starting to pour in for AI programs. Expectations grew. By the 90s, AI, or some form of it, was embedded in a growing number of applications, from machine intelligence to diagnosis of medical problems and detection of credit card fraud, with vast improvements in efficiency and savings for their users. Still, AI stayed pretty much behind the scenes . . . until it beat the world chess champion.

Still At It

More than 60 years after Turing began talking about "artificial intelligence," software developers are still working many of the same issues. After demonstrating prototypes of AI products at the International Joint Conference on Artificial Intelligence in 2001, Microsoft's Bill Gates told the conference that AI was the driver behind several of his company's R&D programs. At the Massachusetts Institute of Technology, where Marvin Minsky, the author of *Society of Minds*, and John McCarthy formed an AI Lab in 1959, lab director Rodney A. Brooks likes to point out that from 1970 to 1990 the peak amount of computer power available for an individual AI researcher remained fairly constant at around 1 million instructions per second. "Since 1990," Brooks says, "we have picked up more than two orders of magnitude processing for individual graduate students. In addition, much larger central computational systems are becoming available for dedicated experiments, giving yet another order of magnitude increase."

British physicist Stephen Hawking suggests that the only way humans will be able to keep up with the current pace of technological development is to improve themselves through genetic engineering. Hawking told the news magazine *Focus* that science could "improve" human beings but that it wouldn't be an easy process. With computers pretty much doubling their performance every 18 months, Hawking said, "We should follow this road if we want biological systems to remain superior to electronic ones. The danger is real that they [computers] could develop intelligence and take over the world."

Are today's computers powerful enough to demonstrate real intelligence? MIT's John McCarthy says on his MIT Web site that some people think that much faster computers are required for them to be truly intelligent. McCarthy believes that the computers of 30 years ago were fast enough; we just didn't know how to program them.

How long will it take to close the gap between human and artificial intelligence? Ray Kurzweil, a recognized AI pioneer and winner of the 1999 National Medal of Technology, has been playing around with this stuff since he was 12; he says maybe another 30 years. Retired Intel Corp. Chairman Gordon Moore is slightly more optimistic, at least when it comes to such applications as AI-level speech recognition, which would require computers, among other things, to consistently understand the difference between, say, the word "baker" (the occupation) and "Baker" (someone's name). He thinks that will take only about another 20 years.

TRUE STORY

Remember HAL, the talkative and alarmingly intelligent computer in the high-flying science fiction flick of the 1960s, *2001: Space Odyssey*? Of all the names that Arthur C. Clarke could have come up with, why HAL?

What letters follow H, A, and L in the alphabet?

Clarke claims it is pure coincidence. What do you think?

Playing (Wireless) Games

Any significant growth in revenue from mobile commerce (m-commerce) isn't expected to occur until sometime after 2004. But there are a few spots for wireless carriers that hold more immediate promise. One of these is entertainment—particularly electronic games.

According to The Strategis Group, which publishes market research on high-tech industries, online entertainment through cellular phones and other wireless devices already leads all other m-commerce types of transactions, accounting for more than a third (34%) of the total in 2001—well ahead of shopping and stock trading at 20% each. This follows a strong showing in 2000 in which the sale of electronic games nearly matched movie box-office receipts. Which explains why wireless device manufacturers are adding games to their newest product designs. PDA, cellular phone, and even pager manufacturers now offer a variety of games and other types of entertainment (new movie trailers, for example), some capable of being downloaded into their wireless devices. Nokia has created a Mobile Entertainment Service to help online content publishers develop Web-enabled games for Nokia's wireless devices. With more than 300 companies registering for the program, Nokia expects 30% of its revenue to come from mobile entertainment by the end of 2003. Activision is converting its already well-positioned Hitchhiker's Guide to the Galaxy into a WAP-ready game. Motorola has teamed with gamemaker Sega Enterprises to create entertainment software for cellphones, pagers, and PDAs. Another Motorola partner is U.K.-based Digital Bridges, a specialist in single- and multiple-game wireless devices.

Sony, which has already sold millions of its PlayStation 2 games, is working with AvantGo to enable handheld device users to download Jeopardy! from the AvantGo.com mobile portal. Another heavy hitter in the electronic game world, Nintendo, has designed its next-generation Game Boy to connect to a digital cellular phone through the Internet. And America Online (AOL) has teamed with leading software maker Electronic Arts to offer games that run on portable devices. Europe, it turns out, is at least as hot a market for games, with the U.S. Paris-based Bouygues Telecom providing Short Messaging Service (SMS) and WAP-based games to wireless users. Two other French companies, Fusio and Weraska, are also developing WAP-enabled games, one of which uses real-time traffic mapping services.

Sony Pictures Digital Entertainment has found a way to promote its games and movies at the same time. Sony has taken what it calls "advergaming" from the desktop to handheld devices with the launch of an interactive PDA-based game to promote Revolution Studios & Columbia Pictures' *The One*. According to Sony, this is the first time that a studio has created a PDA-based game on behalf of a major motion picture release. Geoffrey Ammer, president of marketing for Sony Pictures Entertainment, provided the hype: "The thematic elements of *The One* fit perfectly with the idea of a PDA-based game. This is a great way to get the storyline of the movie out and pave the way for users to have an even more enhanced movie-going experience."

TRUE STORY

Back in the 1970s, when Data General Corp. and Digital Equipment Corp. were flying high as the biggest suppliers of "minicomputers" for business and scientific applications, an industry friend of mine came up with what he thought was a pretty good idea. He wanted to install one of these computers in just about every hospital in the world and dedicate it to electronic games. Every patient would have a terminal tied into the computer. If patients on the fourth floor in the west wing of a hospital wanted to play chess with other mid-level players on the second floor of the east wing, they could do it. Or backgammon. Or hundreds of other games. They could do this without ever meeting each other.

To pay for this system, the hospitals would charge each patient a small fee, just like they do for the TV set in their room. In time, the system would more than pay for itself. The technology was in place. The game people were very interested. The problem was the hospitals. No matter how hard he pitched the idea, none of them were willing to make the up-front investment in a PDP-11 or any other minicomputer available at the time. Some said they simply didn't want to be in that business, others didn't believe there would ever be a payback. So, it never happened.

Not a fun place, hospitals.

5

Growing the
Internet (Wirelessly)

Anyone old enough to remember the movie, The Graduate, will recall that the star, Dustin Hoffman, is told at his college graduation party to keep one word in mind when considering a career—"plastics." If that movie were made today, or even a few years ago, plastics would have been supplanted by "wireless" or "the "Internet." Or both.

Today, well over half of U.S. households have Internet access. By 2005, 75% of U.S. households are expected to be connected. Summary statistics published by the Federal Communications Commission in August 2001 show that high-speed lines linking homes and businesses to the Internet increased by 63% during the second half of the year 2000, climbing to a total of 7.1 million. The rate of growth for the full year was 158%. Worldwide, about 430 million people had access to the Internet at the end of 2001. That number will climb significantly when everyone carrying a cellular phone or a wireless-enabled

PDA can access the Net. Indeed, the only thing receiving more buzz today than the Internet and wireless is the wireless Internet. And while each is doing extremely well, together they are struggling.

• • •

Expectations are huge. And that's part of the problem. In 1997, Nortel Networks said the wireless Internet was poised to open the door to a new world of advanced network services, with the next wave of mobile computing capabilities including on-the-move Internet and intranet access, graphics-enabled e-mail, file transfers, and "off the shelf" IP push applications.

Poised may not have been the right word, but it hasn't slowed the hype. "In the past 10 years," Rich Templeton, Texas Instruments' COO, said in a news release issued by TI in August 2001, "we've seen beyond a doubt that the Internet is the future of information technology, and looking forward, mobility is the future of the Internet. Wireless phones outsold PCs for the first time last year, and virtually all analysts agree that within the next few years, portable Internet appliances will become the preferred tools for Internet access on a global basis."

The wireless industry's vision is that the Internet will increasingly go wireless and that people will regularly be acquiring data with wireless handsets and mobile appliances. But with wireless data accounting for barely more than 5% of all wireless traffic, the industry clearly has its work cut out for it in finding a pricing plan that will attract new customers and in raising consumer awareness about the wireless Internet. You knew things weren't going as well as planned when *Technology Review* published a feature in June 2001 under the headline "Mobile Web Vs. Reality."

The problem, Brad Smith wrote in the November/December 2001 issue of *Wireless Internet* magazine is that "the wireless Internet industry has a bad case of the 'tomorrows.' We always hear things like 'this will take off when networks have the band-width to support it.' Well, waiting for tomorrow is the kind of business plan that put a number of wireless data companies out of business in 2001." Smith's suggestion is don't wait. "Other-wise," he says, "the wireless Internet will always be tomorrow."

iMarketing News didn't help when it reported in its April 2, 2001 issue, "Despite the hype of the wireless Internet and 3G services, wireless providers have not yet offered consumers compelling reasons to go online via cellphones and mobile devices."

The most critical issue facing the industry is developing new and compelling wireless data applications. Compelling is important. What's the point of coming up with new things if no one wants to use them?

TRUE STORY

It was about 1977. I took a call while trying to make a noon deadline for my *Consumer Electronics Daily* newsletter. It was some guy in Chicago . . . said he was a graduate EE student and he wanted to tell me about his new "invention." He also needed my advice about how to get it manufactured. He said he wanted to make some "serious money" out of this thing. Sounded interesting enough for me to stop what I was doing and listen.

He described his invention as a portable device that looked very much like a Motorola pager, but it wasn't really a pager. In fact, it didn't actually receive any radio signals of any kind. But it did have a hidden button that made the device beep like a pager after about a 45-second delay.

"What's the point of this device?" I asked.

"It's great in singles bars," he said. "You can pretend you're a doctor. It really impresses the ladies." Or, he elaborated, you can get out of boring meetings. Simply press the hidden button when no one is looking, place your hands on the table so you're not so obvious and wait for the beep. Then, you excuse yourself from the meeting, explaining that you have been waiting for this "important call."

I forget what I told him, but I never heard from him again. Or his invention.

Who Needs It?

Several analysts have predicted that wireless banking would take off almost immediately. According to the 2001 Consumer Survey, a joint survey of American Banker and the Gallup Organization, however, 78% of the respondents who own or use a cellular phone or PDA said they have no interest in doing financial transactions wirelessly. Only 22% expressed any interest in using their wireless devices for banking or other financial applications. Analysts attribute this lack of interest to "dashed expectations," meaning that consumers expect the same kind of performance out of the wireless Internet that they get when sitting at home or in their office working on their desktop PCs. Interfaces, such as keyboards, are too small to do any effective work on most portable devices. And the screens are too small to handle any meaningful information. Wireless Web browsers, despite recent improvements, don't offer the same Net access and navigation experience as a PC. At least, not yet.

The market intelligence firm International Data Corp. expects the number of wireless subscribers in the United States to increase at an impressive compound annual growth rate of 73%; that's up from approximately five million in 2000 to more than 84 million in 2005. IDC believes the uptake will begin to seriously kick in beginning in 2003 with a boost from three key developments:

- Wireless data rates will be faster than landline dial-up rates as carriers roll out their 2.5 Generation and Third-Generation networks.
- More functional end-user equipment designed for wireless Internet usage will become available in mass-market quantities in 2003 and 2004.
- The always-on capabilities of the news devices and improved applications will drive usage of the wireless Web.

An Optical Illusion

In the early 1990s, telecom carriers thought they had a new revenue stream with another broadband technology—optical fiber—and tried to push it into consumers' homes. To help lure consumers, the telcos pitched such killer applications as voice-on-demand and interactive TV. It simply wasn't enough to get enough consumers to bite. Again, the assumption that "If you build it, they will come" didn't work.

The tough nut that comes out of a survey by Parks Associates is that Internet consumers are simply not willing to pay

$45 to $50 a month for high-speed service. Speed is not enough, even if it means much more compelling content and quicker downloads. Most Parks' survey respondents said their slower dial-up service was "good enough" for their needs. The numbers have to be scary for broadband marketers—71.3% of Parks' respondents were very satisfied, moderately satisfied, or somewhat satisfied with their dial-up Internet service, while only a total of 16% said they were somewhat, moderately, or not at all satisfied with this service.

Real-world experience seems to support the data. As the *Chicago Tribune* put it in its November 12, 2001 edition, "Those in the computer industry who devise high-tech gadgets for mass markets are confronting what to them is an unthinkable possibility; the average consumer may not want a super-fast connection to the Internet." Major wireless carriers such as AT&T, Sprint, SBC Communications, the *Trib* discovered, were beginning to pull back from their aggressive broadband marketing campaigns. At the same time, two major industry groups—the Telecommunications Industry Association and the Information Technology Association of America—warned of waning consumer interest in high-speed networking if tax credits and other changes aimed at promoting broadband deployment to American homes were not instituted. The "general indifference [to broadband services] by consumers," the *Trib* reported, "has alarmed the industry."

This could change, especially as prices drop, but several surveys indicate that few consumers—at least very few American consumers, unlike business users—are willing to pay a premium for additional speed. In fact, some market analysts, such as Jupiter Media Metrix, expect more than 40% of U.S. households to be accessing the Internet at higher speeds by 2006. Jupiter's reasoning is that once people are exposed to the benefits of broadband, they will more seriously consider switching to the higher-speed, higher-cost service.

What's the rush? Equipment and service providers believe that most people will need and want their products and services. Ericsson and others put these products and services in three categories. The first comes under mobile commerce (banking, trading, ticketing, and shopping); the second, mobile-WWW (browsing/video and audio streaming for information, such as news, sports, entertainment, and navigation services). And finally, there's mobile messaging, including e-mail, voice mail, Short Messaging Services (SMS), video/imaging, and instant messaging.

More (or Less) Online Shopping

Then there's the slowdown in online shopping. Jupiter says there were 39.3 million online buyers in 2000, representing 34% of the online population. At the end of 2000, Jupiter projected that number would climb to 85 million in 2003, an estimate it probably based to some extent on the triple-digit growth rates of 1996 to 2000. But by the second quarter of 2001, that number had slipped to 24.7%, according to the U.S. Commerce Department, when several key players dropped out of the business.

A negative press may be part of the reason for the slip in interest in online shopping. The Internet popped into the Top 10 list of consumer complaints published by the National Association of Consumer Agency Administrators and the Consumer Federation of America for the first time, sharing eighth place with complaints about mail order shopping, telemarketing, and problems with landlords and tenants—but still well ahead of grievances about auto repair. The biggest problem, according to reports from 45 federal, state, and local consumer agencies who participated in the survey, is that people don't always get what they order when they shop online and sometimes don't get anything at all.

Some of the high-tech PR firms promoting the Internet and wireless may unwittingly be part of the problem. An online study conducted by LeFile.com came up with the conclusion that when it comes to making the best use of their own Web sites to market themselves, not one of these firms has hit a home run. LeFile said it based its review of the PR firms on simple, everyday Web-use criteria—the time it takes for the homepage to download with a 56K modem, clear identification of the media or marketing e-mail contacts of the PR firms, the presence of press releases and news coverage about the firms, and client work case histories or other information about the firm's achievements. Since most Web visitors leave a site if not satisfied in less than 30 seconds, the time it takes to get content on the screen is critical. Not one of the firms surveyed by LeFile scored a perfect 10, and two got a zero in this category for glitz that caused load time to exceed a minute or more.

Instead of info@firm, LeFile looked for a real name attached to an e-mail address. Only four firms scored perfectly. Some had no e-mail addresses at all. The study also found that three firms listed no press releases of its coverage by the media and only four presented any sort of media coverage of their work. Case histories of actual client projects or other real examples of how the firm works can be tasty fodder for marketing and publicity. But only half of the firms scored 10s in this category, while three had no examples.

The Dot-Com Bomb

By itself, the death of so many dot-com companies and the coverage of these failures in such a short period of time was painful enough. According to WebMergers, a consulting group that tracks Internet-related companies, 716 dot-coms closed between January 2000 and mid-November 2001. In the same period, more than 1,000 were acquired.

Even more troubling, perhaps, Harris Interactive found in a survey in the fall of 2001 that the proportion of all adults who are online at work, at home, or any other location (cyber cafes, libraries, schools) has remained virtually unchanged at 64% for the previous 12 months. This translates into about 127 million adults aged 18 and over, up from 121 million in the previous year. What is remarkable about these results is that this is the first time since the Internet began its rapid growth in 1994 that there has not been a sizeable increase in Internet penetration over a 12-month period. The proportion of all adults online was 9% in 1995. It rose to 30% in 1997, to 56% by 1998, and to 63% by the fall of 2000. The one percentage point increase from 2000 to 64% in 2001 is statistically insignificant. Another trend tracked by the Harris poll shows 73% of all adults using a computer at home, work, or some other location. This number is also virtually identical to the 74% reported in 2000.

Harris offers only two possible reasons for this slowing rate of Internet growth. For one thing, the weakening economy could be inhibiting Internet penetration. Another possible factor is that the rapid growth of the Internet appears to have stopped at, or around, the crash of the Internet stocks on the NASDAQ.

Through all this, businesses continue to increase their spending on developing Internet-and wireless-related activities. And with an estimated 25 million small businesses in the United States and only five million of them on the Internet at the end of 2001, there's a long way to go to grow the technology—and the market.

Chris Larsen, president and CEO of Pacific WebWorks, put a good, local spin on the dot-com demise in a news release. His company develops software that helps small- and medium-sized companies build, manage, and maintain Web sites, sell products, and collect information about Web visitors. "Over the past year, there has been a lot of press about dot-com failures, but if you consider what happened when other dramatic technologies emerged, like the railroads, the recent Internet shakeout is not surprising. And it is important to remember that good, solid, sensible approaches are surviving, that's the reason Pacific WebWorks has weathered the storm."

Still, just about everyone is still high on the potential for dot-coms—as long as the niche is right, such as travel. And even as many of the dot-coms fade, surveys by DiamondCluster International, a business and technology strategies consultancy, and the Wharton School of the University of Pennsylvania, indicate that 70% of senior executives rank Internet technologies as either "important" or "essential" to their core business success and that the positive effects of the Internet are only now beginning. The survey's clear message is that any company that doesn't transform itself around this technology will be left behind.

The dot.com fallout has also reached publications that have routinely publicized and promoted these companies and others. Several newspapers have killed their technology sections for lack of advertising. The *Dallas Morning News* dropped its weekly Personal Technology section. Gannett, the newspaper chain, folded its free-standing "*e*" section on consumer tech into its business sections. The *Toronto Star* killed its six-year-old Fast Forward section and the *Houston Chronicle* closed its two-year-old tech section. The *Orange County Register* dropped Connect, its two-year-old tech supplement. Also gone are several magazines, including *Industry Standard*, and *On*, which used to be *Time Digital*, the magazine covering the benefits of consumer technologies that AOL Time Warner launched in 2000 and redesigned a year later. Also, *FamilyPC* and *Business 2.0*, whose motto was "New Economy—New Rules—New Leaders." Ziff-Davis Media merged its *Interactive Week* with *eWeek*.

It's tough getting the word out when you can't afford the paper to print it on.

The Digital Divide

Despite lower-cost PCs and phenomenal growth in the Internet, there is still a strong Digital Divide in the United States. Translated, this means that, for various reasons, everyone doesn't have the same access to information technology and other telecom and computer services. To narrow this divide, Gartner Dataquest thinks the government will have to play a more active role. "Governments need to encourage business strategies that help to narrow the Digital Divide," says Gartner. "Government policies such as tax credits for providing Internet access to employees and telecommuting can encourage businesses to provide low-cost Internet access for workers in their homes."

According to Gartner, three major factors prolong the Digital Divide in the United States. One is access to the Internet in the home. While more than half of U.S. households have Internet access, the penetration rate differs drastically based on socioeconomic status, which is a combination of household income and education level. In late 2000, Gartner research showed that 35% of the lowest socioeconomic status Americans had Internet access, compared to 53% in the lower-middle socioeconomic bracket, 79% in the upper-middle bracket, and 83% in the highest socioeconomic bracket.

Then, there's broadband. While Internet penetration is expected to surpass 75% of U.S. households by 2005, another Digital Divide emerges, stemming from high-speed access through bandwidth. Even if Internet access to the home advances with a higher level of penetration, a new Digital Divide will, as Gartner put it, "gape before us if broadband access costs an additional $40 per month per household. This will be the equivalent of having the moderate and upper classes in iMAX theatres while the underprivileged are still watching silent movies." The third factor is what Gartner calls the Experimental Divide. Once online, users have a ramp-up period of several months to several years before they fully realize the benefits of the Internet. Becoming Internet-proficient is a skill acquired over time.

And time will tell.

6

Future Hype

No matter what anyone tells you, the future is unclear. And that includes the near future.

Everything is moving too fast. Every portable electronic device (and some not-so-portable devices) you purchase will be out of date in six months. But this has been pretty much the case for years. Technology journalists used to joke that video war games sold in consumer electronics stores were more sophisticated than most of the flight simulators used by military pilots to practice low-altitude dog fights and bombing runs. But it was true. The Pentagon's purchasing process simply doesn't allow for the acquisition and deliv-

ery of new and emerging technologies that come anywhere close to what happens in the real world. The fact is, consumers have first crack at just about everything.

Computers, communications, and consumer electronics have already converged into consumers' pockets and purses. Connectivity is pervasive. The long-predicted "post-PC" era is already an entrenched, but still evolving, global trend. "For many people in the world," J. Gerry Purdy, the CEO of Mobile Insights, a Silicon Valley-based consulting firm, wrote in his newsletter, "the only experience with the Internet will be through a wireless handheld device." IBM agrees. It projects that mobile Internet solutions and services will become an $83 billion market by 2003, with one billion wireless subscribers.

Arthur D. Little, Inc., the Boston-based management and technology consulting firm, says that 86% of the respondents to one of its surveys believe that wireless will overtake landline service within a decade—19% expect the change to occur by 2006. An ADL competitor, McKinsey & Co., in a "Going Mobile" brief it published in 2000, wasn't surprised that wireless service providers see the residential voice traffic now carried mainly on landlines as an alluring source of future growth. "If 50% of the voice traffic now handled by Europe's residential landline networks moved to mobile ones, usage on most of them would double or even triple."

Even if the wireless Internet isn't growing as fast as anticipated, it eventually will outpace fixed telecom lines simply because Americans love their mobility and wireless and the Internet will continue to converge into every kind of conceivable product. It's about never being out of touch. By 2003, at least 75% of all wireless phones will be Web-enabled.

Obeying the Law

You probably have heard about Moore's Law. In 1965, now retired Intel Chairman Gordon Moore predicted in an interview with *Electronics* magazine that semiconductor capacity would double about every 18 months. And it has. In a more recent interview with *EE Times*, Moore was asked about where he saw technology going over the coming years. "My visibility has usually been limited to the next couple of generations of technology. That's six years or so for you to see what's going to happen technically. Even then it's hard to see where the big impacts are going to come from. I calibrate myself by saying [that] if you'd asked me in 1980 what the big impact of microprocessors would be, I probably would have missed the PC. If you asked me in 1990 what was important, I probably would have missed the Internet."

The *push* provided by rapidly advancing technologies has resulted in an expanded set of demands that are *pulling* the development of a growing number and variety of applications. Consumers and business managers and professionals have their own specific needs, particularly in mobile computing and communications, which is complicated by the fact that each new product seems to be faster, smaller, and lighter, with more features than its predecessor.

Product obsolescence has almost ceased being an issue. A friend has three daughters, four years apart in age. In her early teens, he bought the first daughter a record player. He bought the second one a tape deck. The third daughter got a CD player. They're all now downloading music off the Internet. Most professional commercial photographers accept that they will soon be shooting everything in a digital format. Camcorders have replaced 8mm and 16mm film movie cameras, even though consumers know that the video camcorder they're purchasing will be larger and heavier and have fewer features than the "new" line that will be introduced in six months. Handheld TVs are getting smaller, even as their screens are getting slightly bigger and sharper—and they're in color.

As reported in the *New York Times*, Clifford Nass, a professor of communications at Stanford University, sees this phenomena in social terms. The problem, he says, is that technologies change faster than people can adapt to them. Companies struggle with how often to upgrade their PCs. Most people keep their TV sets for at least 10 years, eventually relegating them to a back bedroom before replacing them with a new set. Because they keep getting smaller and lighter and are a personal device with lots of new features, cellular phones

© 2000 Ted Goff

"As you can see, reality is going up,
and will soon overtake our hype."

don't last nearly that long; consumers usually exchange their old models for new ones every 18 to 21 months. Curiously, what most consumers consider to be some of the most important features in their high-tech portable products receive little promotional attention from manufacturers. These include miniaturization, batteries, and ease of use.

Miniaturization

Can "portable" consumer electronic products possibly get any smaller? They can and they will. Today, more than ever, personal electronics have to be small to make it big in today's market.

Every survey conducted in the past few years indicates that only cost is more important to consumers than the size and weight of their cellular phone. In fact, the words "small" and "smaller" appear frequently in both consumer technology and technical publications, a testament to the pressure that engineers are under to further shrink their newest designs.

One of the key factors pushing the development of wireless and portable consumer electronics is the rapidly shrinking size of electronic components. So much so that China-based phone manufacturer FTIC Capital is using components developed by

Agere Systems (formerly the Lucent Technologies' Microelectronics Group) to produce two Internet-enabled cellphones that are 30% smaller than a business card and weigh only about 2.4 ounces, or about 70% lighter than most wireless handsets. The RF (radio frequency) identification ring developed by Dallas Semiconductor so that its employees can access secure areas by emitting a coded signal is another example of what is possible with miniature devices. Digital watches also have gained new functionality as pagers, electronic organizers, traffic reporters, e-mail receivers, and cameras in the last few years.

System-on-a-chip technology has enabled more functionality to be integrated into a single chip and at higher speeds, reducing the overall size and even battery consumption of portable electronics. But chips are no longer the limiting factor in reducing the size of many of today's new products—the problem, it turns out, is the people who use them. The keyboards are too small to easily type on. The displays are too small to be read or to display any useful information. Voice recognition is the obvious choice to replace, or even eliminate, the tiny keypads in cellular phones, but that technology still doesn't work as advertised. An exception was the working digital watch/phone demonstrated by Nippon Telegraph & Telephone Co. during the 1998 Winter Olympics in Japan. The prototypes had four buttons, with most of its operation handled by a built-in voice recognition system. Samsung produced a wristwatch mobile phone, which it demonstrates mostly at trade shows; like the NTT device, it is a concept model and has not yet reached the market.

AT&T produced a working Dick Tracy-like concept wrist phone about five years ago that wasn't much bigger than many of today's multifeatured digital watches. It had dual wristbands. A bell sounded when the phone/watch received a call. The wearer automatically took the phone "off the hook" by pressing down on the top of the watch. This released an outer band that contained the speaker. The miniature speaker pivoted into the wearer's palm so that he or she could cup a hand over an ear and speak into the wrist unit. When the call was completed, the speaker band could be snapped back into place over the wristband.

A wireless phone in a pen or built into your eyeglasses? You have been seeing too many Wesley Snipes and James Bond movies. (It's just a matter of time.)

Battery Technologies

The outlook is for more advanced batteries and, therefore, better-performing portable products. However, in the short term, much of the improvement in battery drain will actually come from new microprocessors, not from any deficiencies in the battery technology itself. Powering today's portable electronic products will continue to frustrate users who, according to just about every consumer survey ever taken, want their batteries to "last forever," at least for a while. Meanwhile, some totally new technologies, including zinc-air and fuel cells, are emerging.

Batteries that are used to power cellular phones (cellphones seem to be a good present-day example) are heavy and limited in their hours of operation, frustrating engineers who have been trying every possible technical trick to reduce the size, weight, and shape of their product designs, as well as consumers who increasingly are confronted by new phones with features that allow them to do a lot more than just talk.

Cellphone manufacturers promote the talk time and standby time of their cellphone models, but very few publish data indicating to what extent add-on features, such as FM radios, games, MP3, and wireless data applications deplete their batteries. NTT DoCoMo, Japan's largest wireless carrier, got high marks when it began field-testing its new video-enabled Third-Generation (3G) Freedom of Mobile Access phone. The one complaint from consumer/testers: Set in the call-waiting mode, the new phone had to be recharged almost daily.

The Portable Rechargeable Battery Association won't disclose the size of the market because its member companies forbid the association from talking about industry sales, even cumulatively. But it's huge. Independent studies indicate that cellular phones now consume well over 60% of the so-called 3Cs (portable computers, cellular phones, and video camcorder) segment of the U.S. rechargeable battery cell market.

More-complex applications demand more battery power, and designers are working overtime to find every little power-saving trick they can think of, from using screen savers and sleep modes to creating low-power states in the internal electronics of portable phones during pauses in conversations.

The Arthur D. Little survey mentioned earlier also identified battery technology as a key component in enabling next-generation technology. "We are seeing the battery industry continue to be pushed towards developing technology for the production of long-lasting, smaller batteries," says Christina Lampe-Onnerud, director of battery technology at ADL's Technology and Innovation Department.

Several developments that are underway should help. Nickel metal hydride (NiMH) batteries are still a staple of many portable products, but lithium ion (L-ion) batteries, which have greater energy density and are becoming more cost competitive with NiMH, are gaining market share. The more advanced lithium polymer batteries, which are lighter and thinner and promise even better battery life, are now reaching the market. Lithium polymers also give product designers some design flexibility. Another plus for these batteries (and product designers) is that they don't require a metal can, but can be molded to fit the product without the shape limitations of other battery technologies. And they're light: 0.88 lbs. for those now available as an option for Sharp Electronics' notebook computers.

Another solution is zinc-air batteries, which draw oxygen from the atmosphere to extend their life. Electric Fuel Corp. has introduced a "ready to use" zinc-air cell designed specifically for all popular models of video camcorders. Electric Fuel says that its new "breakthrough product" eliminates the need for camcorder users to wait for rechargeable batteries to complete their charging cycle, providing up to 10 hours of shooting using the same power source. Another new development is chip-controlled and rechargeable "smart battery" packs that communicate their status to the host product, as well as providing performance data.

With a Little Bit of Luck . . .

The newest "next generation" battery development is fuel cells, which use pollution-free hydrogen gas to generate electric current, but they're still at least a few years off for portable electronic devices. With any luck, they may catch the end of the Third-Generation (3G) cellphone wave. 3G phones will require more power for improved and bigger displays, more features, and faster data transfer. Most of the engineering work with fuel cells will focus on chemistries (and there are several choices), miniaturization (higher energy density doesn't help if it doesn't fit into the small, light, portable products that consumers demand), and cost (current fuel cell prototypes are expensive; one of challenges will be taking much of the front-end engineering cost out of this technology before trying to introduce it as a consumer product). But news of the ongoing development of fuel cells will find its way into the consumer and technical press while engineers try to advance the technology.

Fuel cells received a huge PR boost toward the end of 2001 when *Time* magazine named as one of its Inventions of the Year a prototype bicycle designed by Aprilia S.p.A. and powered by a fuel cell produced by Manhattan Scientific, Inc.'s NovArs unit in Germany. The Aprilia fuel cell bicycle has a range of slightly over 50 miles. The fuel cell itself weighs less than two pounds. The refueling of the hydrogen container can be done in a minute and the fuel cell system can be produced in large quantities relatively inexpensively, meaning that an entry into the Asia market is a viable possibility. An estimated 10 million noisy, polluting scooters were sold in China in 2000 and an estimated three million in India. So, we will be hearing more about fuel cells.

Wearable computers and communications devices may actually force designers to consider highly innovative power sources. One possibility being advanced is body heat. Another is to use the simple, mechanical energy of walking as a power source.

Little tweaks to the electronics by designers will help, but no near-term solutions are just around the corner for significantly improving the battery life of multifunctional/multifeatured portable devices.

Ease of Use

Are VCRs really so hard to program that no one uses them for anything other than playing rented movies?

You would think so—unfortunately. Technology journalists have been editorializing for years about the need to simplify the use of PCs. A similar call has gone out for portable wireless devices, including cellular phones, and other portable electronic products. At its most practical level, adding e-mail and Internet service to wireless devices has become a major task in trying to enable users to navigate the tiny keyboards and read the skimpy pieces of information that show up on the tiny screens of portable devices.

Even what used to be familiar is becoming more complicated. Consumers and business users throughout the United States now have to go through 10-digit dialing—the area code *and* the phone number—to allow for additional area codes. In some case, this means reprogramming personal hardware and services, such as speed-dialing computer modems, automatic dialers, cellular phones, security systems, pagers, fax machines, home voice mail or answer call, call forwarding, and PBX business phone systems that dial local phone numbers. For "simplicity's sake," Verizon Wireless said in a news release, "calls dialed using '1' before the 10-digit number will always go through, whether it's a local, toll, or long distance call."

Researchers at Stanford University, claiming that the depersonalization of communications technology is turning the people who use it into "outsiders," are trying to figure out how to make software more appealing to consumers and easier to use. To help things along, a Stanford team is working on a new "mobile people architecture," essentially a new software platform it believes will provide more personalized services without adding to the complexity of the network infrastructure, making new features more human-centric rather than focusing on the technology itself.

One of the messages that IBM passed along to its audience at the 1999 Conference on Pervasive Computing, which it sponsored with the Industrial Design Society of America, was that the next stage of the computer revolution will be to make technology simpler and more reliable, with the complexity hidden from the user. Its goal, IBM said, was to make the infrastructure invisible. But two years later, Microsoft's Bill Gates, in his 2001 keynote speech at COMDEX, the always massive U.S. computer trade show, said it would take at least a few more years for home wireless networking and high-speed Internet to reach most U.S. homes. "It's got to be a lot easier than it is today," Gates said.

Sketches of coffeemakers with remotely controlled touch-screen control pads and toasters with digital displays reading, "You've got mail," began to appear more frequently in the mass media in the late 1990s, but these products aren't likely to be available any time soon. For one thing, it's not clear that anyone wants them. And that's largely the issue: They represent an immature technology and overinflated expectations. And does anyone really need a refrigerator that tells them they're almost out of milk?

Hoping to support its case for an easier, cheaper, and more reliable form of wireless communications, Arch Wireless Corp. commissioned the Sag Harbor Group to study the strengths of its messaging technology over more complex and highly integrated voice and data devices offered by major wireless carriers as they migrate through 2.5 Generation into Third-Generation (3G) systems. The result was a 70-page white paper suggesting that U.S. consumers are being "seduced" into accepting the promises of next-generation wireless products and services, including streaming video and the high-speed Internet.

Arch's fear of failure was well founded: As the Sag Harbor study anticipated, a number of U.S.-based two-way messaging device manufacturers exited the business, forcing networks to look to European and Asian production sources.

A Real Learning Experience

Even though three-quarters of the nation's schools were wired and online by 1999, teachers were still struggling with how to use the technology in the classroom. Today, most states require computer education for teachers. Nevertheless, more than 60% of the K–12 teachers surveyed by Market Data Retrieval in 1999 said they were "not at all prepared" to integrate technology into the classroom.

One idea that a number of industry analysts and even a few phone manufacturers and wireless carriers were promoting not too many years ago just as dual-mode (analog and digital) phones were hitting the market, was an analog-only cellphone for people who wanted to keep it real simple. All they wanted was a cheap phone and cheap service. They only wanted to talk. But that idea didn't get very far. Today's minimalist wireless subscriber may still have to purchase a dual-mode/tri-band cellphone with additional features.

Battery-Powered People

"Smart clothes" is another next new thing—it's in quotation marks because it hasn't yet reached the level of market maturity to be called, simply, smart clothes. Jokes about needing a Batman-like utility belt to carry all of your high-tech toys are no longer very funny. At least not for the consumer electronics and computer companies and a few startups that are trying to create a market for "wearable electronics," or "wireless wear." The hype may be at least slightly ahead of the reality, but some e-wear is already available, and more is on the way.

To be sure, there are probably thousands of fashionably designed models of electronic watches on the market with a variety of advanced features, ranging from built-in messaging capability to waterproof wrist devices that scuba divers can hook up to their PCs après dive to produce a graphic representation of their dives (how much time at what depth, etc.). Radios have been built—James Bond-style—into ballpoint pens. Joggers can purchase extremely lightweight AM/FM radios that fit over one ear.

There are also eyeglasses with head-up displays, similar in concept to what fighter pilots see when looking out of their cockpits. Head-up displays would also enable drivers to read maps or directions displayed on the lenses of their eyeglasses while still having full-view of the road ahead.

Commercial head-up displays currently range from $700 at the very low end to $12,000 and higher. The target price for practical consumer use is $50 or less. Of course, the cost will drop with volume production, but display manufacturers still have a long way to go to get the price down, even for early adopters. And despite a fair amount of ink devoted in the consumer technology press, the uptake on these devices has been weak to virtually nonexistent.

Microchips have already been embedded in rings, necklaces, and key chains to provide their wearers with coded, secure wireless (in this case, radio frequency identification, or RFID) links for entering secure areas, including buildings and laboratories.

But these items are old news. The next step is to completely embed the electronics into the fabric of clothing. One example is the Charmed Communicator—a charm-like device with a digital music player and Internet radio that is likely to make its market debut in the next year or two. Shirts and jackets have already been developed and are being tested with flexible circuitry and antennas integrated into clothing. Xybernaut Corp., which has been designing wearable technologies for years, has granted or has pending applications worldwide on mobile/wearable and related computing technologies.

The Defense Advanced Research Projects Agency (DARPA), a generally secretive agency of the U.S. Department of Defense (DoD), has initiated what may be the most ambitious project in this area when in November 2001 it published a request for proposal (an RFP in military parlance) that would initiate a new research program for wearable computers and related technologies. DARPA's program covers five years, starting with an initial two-year "proof of concept" and "technology assessment" phase, followed by a three-year period in which contractors would have to prove e-textile concepts.

DARPA wants to create true e-textiles, such as textile-embedded sensors and circuits and "active yarns." While the DoD agency's focus is on military applications, there are obvious commercial opportunities. Xybernaut has already delivered a wearable device to British Airways to check in passengers while they wait in long lines at London's Heathrow Airport and has begun delivering this belt-mounted, two-pound unit to U.S. airports so that airport security personnel can instantly identify suspicious travelers, based on biometric-face-recognition technologies. The company is also working on a number of classified projects for the DoD.

The International Biometrics Group is now projecting annual revenue for the wearable computer market at $594 million in 2003. The Gartner Group has put wearable computers in its list of four key, emerging-technology trends for the next decade, along with consumer self-service, Web services, and electronics containing information and opinions about purchasable items. By 2007, according to Gartner, more than 60% of the U.S. population in the 15- to 50-year-old age range will carry or wear a wireless computer and communications device at least six hours a day.

Of course, fashion trends change, but the naked truth may turn out to be in a consumer survey conducted in 2001 by the Consumer Electronics Association, which shows that only 16% of U.S. adults are "very interested" in owning a voice-activated cellular phone designed to look like a pin or button, while more than half (53%) are not at all interested in such a device. At the same time, only 13% say they are very interested in a miniature PC that clips to a belt or purse with a screen built into eyeglasses, and 57% are not at all interested.

While some textile and electronics manufacturers are trying to outfit the market, Docker is already ahead of the curve, having introduced the "Mobile Pant," casual-style slacks with several pockets designed to hold—as the company's x-ray vision TV commercials demonstrate—cellular phones, PDAs, and other personal electronic devices.

3G and Thee

Surely, you have heard of the Third-Generation (3G) by now. Cahners' Wireless Dictionary defines it as "The International Telecommunications Union's name for the new third generation global standard for mobile (GSM) telecommunications." As described on Nokia's Web site, 3G is "watching clips from your favorite soap on the train, sending images straight from the field to headquarters for analysis, sharing your Moroccan vacation with your friends—from Morocco, videoconferencing in a taxi." The Wireless Data Forum's definition provides a little more detail, calling it, "The next step in the development of wireless communications. Third-generation systems are expected to provide broadband, high-speed data applications—both fixed and mobile."

Expected may be the operative word. In its February 15, 1998 issue, *Wireless Review* published a nine-page feature under the big and bold headline, "Hype Or Hope." It was a broad discussion of vendors' and analysts' views of what it will take to get the wireless industry to migrate to 3G wireless, the next stage technologically in cellular communications. Their views were mixed, with most vendors taking the high road and most analysts providing the reality check, with one analyst going so far as to suggest that 3G, "as presently conceived, will prove an economic failure."

Not a lot has changed in the past four years. Despite costly research and development and a continuous stream of marketing hype, vendors and carriers have pushed ahead with their 3G programs but are wary of its potential for success. Analysts increasingly wonder out loud if U.S. consumers really want or need—as 3G promises—higher data transmission speeds and such features as full-motion video on a screen that is only slightly bigger than your thumb.

In the fall of 2001, Goldman Sachs published a report called "3G: Time to Get Real" that suggested the industry was underestimating the difficulty in implementing the technology. About a conference on 3G held in Rome and sponsored by Goldman Sachs, the company said, "There was little presented that excited us about the sector. It seems clear to us that investors are unlikely to become excited about 3G until they see whether GPRS [a high-speed enhancement of current cellular networks, usually referred to as 2.5G] is rolled out successfully over the next 12 months."

Strategy Analytics' assessment of 3G's chances of success: "The reality is that 3G networks will not deliver, nor is there pent-up demand for, the interactive multimedia applications that would require data rates in excess of 384 kilobits per second." Equipment manufacturers, on the other hand, see 3G as a can't miss opportunity to take the technology and the market to a new level.

In This Corner

Wireless carriers and equipment manufacturers may have already hyped themselves into a corner, spending billions to develop a 3G infrastructure, to acquire additional spectrum, and to commit to the purchase of new 3G mobile handsets. But it is taking much longer to get to market than they had hoped, partly because of issues that are beyond their control.

Is there, for example, enough spectrum to accommodate the full-service benefits of 3G? Probably not. Are there enough base stations spotted around the country to handle the increased data traffic that is anticipated with the growth of 3G service subscribers? No, there are not, and considering the difficulty many communities are already having approving the siting of new base stations and those "ugly" antennas that tower hundreds of feet into the air, dropped signals and lost data may contribute to giving 3G a bad name.

The headlines aren't very encouraging. "Americans Consider 3G to be Vaporware" appeared over an *Internet.com* feature, and *Network World* published a piece on 3G topped with the warning, "Cingular, Verizon CEOs Caution Against Unrealistic Hype." *Telephony,* the oldest magazine in the telecommunications industry, went with "Wireless companies downplay 3G hype, focus on near-term opportunities" in one of its regular features on 3G. Most damaging perhaps, because of the size and demographics of its audience, was *BusinessWeek's* piece, "All That Money On 3G—And For What?"

A little history:

In the beginning, there was the First Generation (1G) of cellular communications, a common analog service known in the United States as Advanced Mobile Phone Service (AMPS). The 1G system was characterized by two service providers per service area—an A side (the existing wireline carrier) and the B side (a non-wireline, or wireless carrier). In time, the distinction between the two began to blur, at least for consumers.

Although it is an analog service, cellular digital packet data (CDPD) became available for data but was not widely adopted. As traffic on the system grew, carriers and regulators began to realize that it was time to go to the next technological level. This meant digital.

Digital brought improved sound quality and longer battery life to cellular service. It also added two competing U.S.-evolved digital transmission methods—time-division multiple access (TDMA) and code-division multiple access (CDMA), and a European-developed digital cellular transmission network known as the Global System for Mobile Communications (GSM) to the analog AMPS technical standard for cellular communications—designated EIA/TIA-91.

None of these systems are compatible; if you're on one system, you can't talk with someone on another system. Which explains why many of the cellular phones on the market today are dual-mode (analog and digital) so that if you're using a CDMA phone in a TDMA area, your cellphone will automatically and seamlessly default to the analog network. They're also dual-band, meaning they operate on different frequency bands, which is useful if you move between areas covered by different networks. There is also another mobile service called Personal Communications Service (PCS), which is inherently digital and very similar to cellular, except that it operates on a different radio frequency and is not available everywhere in the United States.

Although most people in the United States are still using 2G phones and service, many new cellular subscribers and those upgrading to new phones are moving into what is known as the 2.5 Generation.

The important advantages of 2.5G are faster data access and an "always on" connection to the Internet. That is, once you log on, you're online for the rest of the day. The speed comes from an evolving standard called Enhanced Data Rates for GSM Evolution, or EDGE, which, at 384 kilobits per second (384 Kb/s), is a higher-speed version of the current Global System for Mobile Communications (GSM) digital wireless. EDGE will operate with both General Packet Radio Service (GPRS), an enhancement to existing GSM networks.

Unfortunately, while European wireless carriers were quick to crank up their GPRS networks beginning in June 2000, it took another year for GPRS-enabled cellphones to hit the market and then only two models were available. And these didn't always work as advertised. The problem, according to Dulacher, a U.K.-based market research organization, is that phone manufacturers were very queasy about investing in GPRS-based models for a market they weren't sure actually existed, while the carriers were reluctant to promote their GPRS service without phones to sell.

The future of 3G totally depends on the development and success of 2.5G, which could be around longer than the "long time" projections of analysts and handset manufacturers. One market analyst, ARC Group, is projecting 203 million mobile data subscribers worldwide by the end of 2003, with 68% of these having access to GPRS, and only 12% 3G subscribers. As usual, business users will be the early adopters. In fact, accessing corporate databases is expected to be a critical element in the growth of the GPRS-enabled phone and PDA market.

Improved Internet Access

Essentially, 3G is expected to enhance access to the Internet (the "killer app" after voice) and other new and emerging applications from a mobile phone, wireless PDA, or any other 3G-enabled wireless device. New consumer applications include mobile commerce (ordering airline tickets and books, making hotel and restaurant reservations, checking on concert and movie schedules), using personal financial services (checking your bank account at any time, paying bills remotely), accessing news and information (news and weather, as well as reference-based services), planning travel (access to location-based information services), and pursuing entertainment (playing interactive networked games for single or multiple players, playing CD-quality music, placing bets on sports events). For business users, the key 3G applications are downloadable e-mail and access to corporate information and services. Other frequently mentioned 3G applications are digital still photography and video, file transfers from an intranet, video conferencing, and satellite-based Global Positioning System (GPS) services.

The history of 3G is fraught with international bureaucratic battles and political intrigue. Barely three years after cellular service started in the United States in October 1983, the Geneva-based International Telecommunications Union (ITU) began to take a serious look at the future of global mobile communications. Several different proposals were submitted for International Mobile Telecommunications (IMT-2000), the formal name for the 3G standard. The DECT and TDMA/Universal Wireless Communications organizations submitted plans for the Radio Transmission Technology proposals for IMT-2000 to be TDMA-based, while all other proposals for non-satellite-based solutions were based on CDMA, a much more complex technology developed by Qualcomm, Inc., in the United States.

CDMA has several variants, including wideband CDMA and cdma2000. Wideband CDMA was backed by the European-based GSM players, including the largest infrastructure vendors—Nokia and Ericsson. cdma2000 was backed by the North American CDMA camp, led by Qualcomm.

Much of the work was done at the 1992 ITU-sponsored World Administrative Radio Conference (WARC-92), with just about every country in the world represented. Most of the attention centered on the two gigahertz (2 GHz) frequency range, which had been identified as the likely place to assign future wireless communications. By the end of the conference, 230 megahertz (230 MHz) of spectrum at around 2 GHz was designated on a global basis for terrestrial and satellite communications under what became known as the Future Public Land Mobile Telecommunications System, or FPLMTS.

By the time WARC-95 rolled around, the frequency allocations had to be modified to deal with the fact that certain regions of the world—in this case, the Americas and the Caribbean—could not accommodate the ITU frequency plan and reallocation schedule. Then, the ITU changed its FPLMTS designation to the IMT-2000, which led to the formation of several tightly knit alliances formed by supporters of CDMA, TDMA, or GSM. Each submitted its proposals to the ITU as a global standard. The ITU received four proposals from the United States and others from Japan, South Korea, China, and Europe, as well as the major international satellite services, including Inmarsat and the European Space Agency.

With so much on the line, both economically and politically, the lobbying for these systems was fierce and relentless. But by early 1999, everyone agreed that there was a great deal of progress in meeting the political and commercial requirements of the various regional groups in formulating the 3G Universal Mobile Telephone System (UMTS). By the end of March 1999, Ericcson and Qualcomm had licensed each other's key intellectual property rights and agreed to the ITU's "family of networks" compromise to the various standards proposals.

The outlook for 3G deployment? Most U.S. carriers hope to formally launch their 3G service sometime in 2002, but it won't be true 3G because the technical capability for all 3G features— the bells and whistles that everyone has heard so much about—won't be in place. In fact, some carriers in the United States are still building out their 2G systems. The reality is that 2.5G may dominate the mass market for several years. And if 2.5G isn't a huge success . . . .

TRUE STORY

Sometime in the early 1990s, when Qualcomm was aggressively promoting its proprietary CDMA technology as the "clear choice" for wireless services to the world's carriers and regulators, the company decided to hold a two-day seminar to lay out in great technical detail the advantages of CDMA. The top executives and chief technical officers of several U.S. and foreign wireless carriers, along with some members of the technical press, were invited to attend the meeting, held at Qualcomm's home base in San Diego, California.

The conference included a highly organized demonstration of the system. Qualcomm had equipped several rented luxury cars and late-model panel trucks with its phones and CDMA-based data transmission equipment to impress its visitors. They rode around San Diego, making calls and sending data over Qualcomm-supplied equipment, to anywhere in the world. Everything worked pretty much the way Qualcomm said it would. It worked so well, in fact, that toward the end of the demo, one of the technical journalists uncharacteristically noted out loud how flawlessly the demo was going. "Thank you," said one of Qualcomm's young engineers who was assisting with the demonstration. "I just hope the car rental people don't check their vehicles too closely when we return them."

"Why not?" the journalist inquired.

"You wouldn't believe how many holes we drilled in these things," the engineer said.

And Fourth Generation (4G) Wireless?

Obviously, the future of Fourth Generation (4G) wireless communications depends on what happens with 3G wireless, which is still only a gleam in the eye in all but a few consumers. But a lot of ideas are floating around as to what 4G might look like.

Like 2.5G, which represents a big jump from 2G in transmission speed and features, 4G may have to ease its way into the next generation by making a brief "stop" at 3.5G. 4G would probably embody the key elements of 3G, but at even higher transmission speeds of 20 to 100 megabytes a second. Ericsson and others expect the *next* next-generation of wireless to offer 50 times today's bandwidth. Plus, it will offer new features deemed critical to future applications by both consumers and business/professional users.

It will very likely include several different networking technologies, including wideband CDMA, the 3G standard offered by the International Telecommunications Union by proponents of the European-developed Global System for Mobile Communications (GSM). Also, cdma2000, a 3G wireless technology submitted by the ITU and based on the cdmaOne standard. It will also feature Enhanced Data Rates for GSM Evolution (EDGE), a higher-speed version (at 384 kilobits per second) of the current GSM digital wireless service. Additional features that would be integrated into 4G would be Bluetooth, the short-range (10 meters) cable replacement radio link, and a wireless local area network based on the IEEE 802.11 technical standard.

It's also likely that most 4G devices would receive most broadcast frequencies, and some (if not all) would operate over one or more mobile satellite services, such as Iridium or Globalstar. Another strong possibility is allowing 4G subscribers to listen in on commercial aircraft communications.

Pervasive access to the Internet will be another obvious feature of 4G, which will also have to incorporate software-defined technologies to be able to adapt to any new transmission methods and "over the air" software upgrades and fixes. Adaptive, or so-called "smart" antennas embedded into 4G devices will enable transmission of error-free data over longer distances.

Spectrum is another concern. Data is a capacity hog. Will there be enough spectrum to handle all of the bells and whistles available with 4G wireless? Any serious discussion of 4G also brings up the potential for cognitive radios; that is, portable radios with software based on artificial intelligence concepts capable of performing dynamic spectrum utilization, making it possible for these radios to share frequencies with other users.

How soon will 4G be a reality? "Generations" usually occur in 10-year cycles. Work on wideband CDMA began around 1990 and still isn't commercially available in any significant way. And since 3G is not yet a reality for most people, we won't be seeing 4G for some time. Several major telecom companies, including Alcatel, Ericsson, Nokia, and Siemens, have formed the Wireless World Research Forum to develop 4G technologies. Also, Hewlett-Packard and Japan's leading wireless carrier, NTT DoCoMo, are working together to "explore new mobile concepts" that might lead to 4G multimedia systems. Their plan is to create an architecture, which they call MOTO-Media, to deliver streaming media to mobile devices that make optimal use of network resources. HP and NTT DoCoMo expect to wrap up their joint research by 2003, just about the time that most analysts expect 3G to begin to become a legitimate mass market product. Ericsson, meanwhile, doesn't expect 4G to be up and operating until around 2010 to 2011. With each generation currently clocking about 10 years or so, it likely won't happen before 2012, maybe even later.

What's the rush? It has virtually nothing to do with you, the consumer. NTT DoCoMo, Japan's largest mobile phone operator, had to delay its well-promoted May 2001 3G launch in Tokyo to October when the phones didn't work as advertised. But its chairman said and the *Kyodo News* reported in early in 2001, development of 4G "must be moved forward" in light of the rapid change in the telecommunications business. Instead of launching its 4G service in 2010, as originally planned, NTT DoCoMo is now shooting for 2007.

Technology Fatigue

A survey in 1997 sponsored by Ameritech, the Chicago-based wireless operator, found that very few consumers (8%) have ever heard of TDMA, CDMA, or GSM, the primary technical standards for transmitting and receiving digital cellular phone calls. Most of the survey's respondents (69%) said they didn't care about the technology, as long as it worked. Only 3% said they knew what PCS stands for. And 86% were unclear about the different types of wireless phone service available.

The *New York Times Magazine* devoted an entire issue in 1997 to "What Technology Is Doing To Us." The coverage was generally positive—until the last feature, when the author (admittedly a nontechnical type) described the difficulty of keeping up with new developments and the problems he was having upgrading his computer and "other gizmos."

The *Times* issue was not lost on the industry. Several manufacturers expressed concern at the time that consumers would become more confused with the introduction of increasingly complex digital products. G. Dan Hutcheson, president of VLSI Research, a Silicon Valley research and consulting firm, addressing a technical conference, said the industry was "running the risk of producing more technology than the world can adapt to." Another analyst, John Ledahl, director of the personal communications program at Dataquest, said, "The entrance of PCS [Personal Communications Service, a technology that competes with cellular] operators into the marketplace is causing confusion among some consumers." Tom Engibous, the president and CEO of Texas Instruments, once suggested in a speech that life would be a lot easier if everyone was assigned a personal phone number and that portable phones and wireless networks were designed so that people could simply punch in a *1 when making a phone call, *2 when sending a fax, *3 when calling a cellular phone number, and *4 when accessing the Internet.

In 1998, Carol Luteran, a New York-based freelance writer, wrote in *Embedded Systems Development* magazine: "Today's consumers are spoiled with an array of products designed to be more productive and offer more convenience. However, stress levels are at an all-time high, people are working longer than ever before, and there's a constant, almost urgent need, for faster and faster products. Are these technological advances playing a dichotomous role of good and evil? Is technology making us too productive and victims of information overload?"

All you have to do is look at the Consumer Electronics Association's online primer of Technologies to Watch with its pumped up commentary—targeting an audience (mostly retailers) that is already sold on this stuff—to get some idea of their expectations going into the 2001 International Consumer Electronics Show in Las Vegas. It's a long list. A few examples:

- Bluetooth—"Leading global powerhouses are betting on Bluetooth as an alternative to other wireless technologies."
- Broadband—"New broadband applications could spur a host of brand new services in the marketplace, including video phones, wireless touchscreens, multimedia advertising, virtual real estate shopping and much more."
- Digital Imaging—"Digital video and photography are rapidly changing the way consumers can capture memories and create video statements. Don't miss the latest digital imaging tools."
- Digital Radio—"Get ready for the radio revolution. Digital radio hits the U.S. market in 2001 and will radically change the current radio landscape."

- Digital Set-Top Boxes—"Will the set-top box replace the PC?"
- Digital Television (DTV)—"Consumer interest is strengthening. All signs point to the imminent success of DTV."
- DVD-Audio—"We are on the verge of a new revolution in the musical listening experience driven by advanced digital technology."
- Home Networking—"More than 73 million American homes know about home networking."
- MP3 and Internet Audio—"See how this technology is changing the music industry forever."
- PDAs and Handheld Computing—"With so much versatility, it may be the key enabling technology that plugs consumers into the future."
- Teleworking—"The technology is here, the employees are ready."

Indeed, we are surrounded by technology, engulfed in it—in our homes, our cars, at work, and in our pockets. And it just keeps coming. Everyone will have to learn, and relearn, at some point, how to use a new technology or product just to stay in the game. Meanwhile, cellphones still drop calls. PDAs lose data. PCs still crash. Voice recognition systems have been around for a long time, but they don't work well in a noisy environment.

Gordon Moore's prediction that the performance of transistors would double every 18 months has not only held up for more than 35 years, it may continue to do so for several more years. But sooner or later, most physicists and some engineers believe that silicon chips, the heart of most electronic devices, will be so small that they will have to turn to some other material to boost the performance of electronic products.

It's time to move on to biochips, gallium-nitride semiconductors, autonomic computing, subatomic quantum computers-on-a-chip, and nanowires, those incredibly tiny molecular-scale post-silicon computers not unlike today's transistors, just a lot faster and smaller.

Hold onto your rechargeable batteries—the hype is in.

Technology Timeline

1832—Charles Babbage conceives the first computer, the Analytical Engine, a mechanical calculating machine that is driven by external instructions. But he never actually builds it, mainly because it was virtually impossible at the time to produce the tooling with the necessary precision to build the machine to Babbage's specifications.

1844—Portrait painter Samuel F. B. Morse sends the first telegraph message: "What hath God wrought?"

1861—The telegraph takes over for the Pony Express.

1872—Thomas Edison invents the phonograph.

1876—Alexander Graham Bell receives a U.S. patent for the telephone.

1877—The first telephone company, Bell Telephone Co., is founded.

1895—Gugielmo Marconi sends and receives wireless signals in Italy.

1889—The first public coin telephone is installed in Hartford, Conn., in the Hartford Bank.

1917—Two-way, air-to-ground communications is used for the first time, as was communications between two aircraft.

1920—KDKA in Pittsburgh goes on the air, becoming the first commercial radio station in the United States.

1924—Zenith Electronics Corp. produces the first portable radio.

1927—Philo Farnsworth applies for a patent for electronic television.

1933—Major Edwin Howard Armstrong receives patents for FM radio.

1939—Television is introduced at the New York World's Fair and RCA, General Electric, DuMont, and Philco sell the first television sets. Also, the first experimental FM radio stations goes on the air.

1945—The first programmable computer, called the Electronic Numerical Integrator and Computer (ENIAC) is demonstrated at the University of Pennsylvania. It weighs 30 tons and requires a large room. Also, Arthur C. Clarke suggests the use of geostationary satellites to provide global communications.

1946—The first mobile telephones are introduced.

1947—AT&T Bell Labs physicists William Shockley, John Bardeen, and Walter Bratain announce the invention of the transistor, for which they will win the Nobel Prize in 1956. The transistor was significantly smaller than the tubes it would eventually replace, had no moving parts, required less power, and had no filaments to create heat. Also, this year, AT&T develops the concept for cellular communications.

1948—The first stored-program electronic digital computer successfully executes its first program. Also, 45 rpm and LP records are introduced. Dr. Peter Goldmark, a Hungarian-born physicist who headed CBS Labs, said he invented the LP because he was annoyed at having to interrupt his favorite classical music pieces by changing 78 records in the middle of a performance. And the first computer company, the Eckert-

Mauchly Computer Co., was formed by the inventors of ENIAC.

1954—Color TV broadcasts begin and the first mass-market transistor "pocket radio" is introduced at $49.95.

1957—The USSR launches Sputnik, the world's first space satellite. In response, the U.S. Department of Defense forms the Advanced Research Projects Agency (ARPA). And the 50 millionth Bell telephone is installed.

1958—Stereo records, phonographs, and modems are introduced. Also in 1958, while everyone else at Texas Instruments was on vacation Jack Kilby, a TI engineer (Kilby had not accrued enough time at TI to take a vacation), demonstrated the first working integrated circuit (IC). He won the Nobel Prize in physics for this achievement in 2000.

1959—Texas Instruments develops the first integrated circuit (IC), opening the way for the development of complex logic functions on a chip.

1961—The Federal Communications Commission (FCC) approves FM stereo broadcasting.

1963—Philips Electronics NV introduces the compact audio cassette.

1965—The U.S. Department of Defense's Advanced Research Projects Agency (ARPA) sponsors a study linking two computers, one at MIT, the other in California. Eight-track audio players are marketed for the first time. Also, Hypertext, a method of preparing text to help readers negotiate their way through material, is invented by Ted Nelson.

1966—Xerox sells its first fax machine, the Telecopier. The Federal Communications Commission initiates its first Computer Inquiry to investigate the role of computers and telecommunications.

1968—In what becomes known as the Carterfone Decision (named after Tom Carter, a Dallas-based telecommunications equipment entrepreneur), the Federal Communications Commission rules that non-AT&T equipment can be connected to the AT&T network. Also, the computer mouse is demonstrated for the first time but is not commercialized for another 16 years by Apple Computer for use with the Apple Macintosh.

1969—The ARPANET, the forerunner of the Internet, developed by the Advanced Research Project (now the Defense Advanced Research Project, or DARPA, a research arm of the U.S. Department of Defense), becomes operational. Four-channel stereo tapes and players are marketed for the first time.

1970—The computer floppy disk is developed. The Federal Communications Commission allocates spectrum for cellular communications. AT&T proposes the first high-capacity cellular telephone system.

1971—Intel introduces the first microprocessor, the 4004, the result of an initial attempt to develop an electronic calculator based on a central processing technology Intel had developed that could be built on a single chip. Also, in 1971, Ray Tomlinson, the principal engineer at BBN Technologies, sends the first electronic mail message—to himself—on the U.S. government computer network that would only a few years later become known as the Internet. Tomlinson's system features just 200 lines of computer code and it only allows him to send a message to a mailbox that is located on the same computer as Tomlinson's.

1973—The Internet is invented by the U.S. Department of Defense. And the Ethernet, a local area network, is developed at the Xerox Research Center in Palo Alto, CA for use with the Alto Aloha Network.

1974—Telnet, the first public packet data service, is launched. The International Telegraph & Telephone Consultative Committee creates the first worldwide fax standard, and Motorola releases the first consumer pager.

1975—The Federal Communications Commission allocates spectrum for mobile communications, including cellular. The first Betamax VCR and the first personal computer, Altair 8800, are introduced.

1976—The Federal Communications Commission opens Computer Inquiry II, focusing on differentiating between basic and enhanced services; it eventually rules that only basic service should be regulated. Wang Laboratories introduces the first word processor.

1977—The first compact autofocus cameras appear on the market. Cellular communications developmental systems are authorized in Chicago and Baltimore/Washington, DC; Specialized Mobile Radio dispatch operations begin service in Chicago. AT&T and GTE install the first fiber-optic telephone systems.

1979—Sony introduces the Walkman, the first personal stereo with headphones. Despite being impressed with its design and sound quality, at a suggested retail price of $195, consumer electronics trade press journalists predict it will be a tough sell. In fact, Sony can't keep up with consumer demand and the company's traditional competitors immediately begin producing their own versions of Walkman. Also in 1979, the first cellular network is launched in Japan.

1980—The first electronic voicemail system is installed, enabling consumers to send and receive messages from anywhere without having to actually speak to anyone.

1981—The IBM PC and the first laptop computer are introduced. The Federal Communications Commission adopts final cellular rules, providing for two licenses in each market.

1982—The U.S. Postal Service begins an electronic mail service, E-Com, allowing messages to be delivered by computer—it is abandoned in 1985. The Transmission Control Protocol (TCP) and the Internet Protocol (IP), also known as TCP/IP, are established as the uniform communications system for ARPANET. Sony introduces the first portable CD player, the Discman.

1983—Cellular phone service is introduced in the United States in Chicago, using a Motorola phone. The phone is priced at $3,995 and weighs 2 pounds, although most of the electronics are built into a box designed to fit in the trunk of cars and trucks of subscribers. McKinsey & Co., a management consultancy, apparently discounting the fact that the phones would eventually get smaller and cheaper, tells AT&T, a client, that no more than 900,000 cellphones will be sold in the United States.

1984—The Domain Name System (using .com in network addresses) is introduced. Also in 1984, the CD-ROM is introduced. Apple Computer introduces the Macintosh with a single $1.5 million commercial during the 1984 Super Bowl.

1985—Airfone initiates a nationwide air-to-ground service on several major airlines.

1987—Cellular signs up its one millionth customer.

1989—Nintendo introduces Game Boy.

1990—The World Wide Web (WWW) is born, and digital audio tape (DAT) is introduced.

1991—The United States begins testing high-definition television (HDTV).

1992—Intel introduces the Pentium processor. Also, digital cellular phone service is introduced. The Federal Communications Commission awards Motorola an experimental license to build and launch five low-earth orbit mobile communications satellites, leading to the formation of Iridium, a global network of 77 (the atomic number for Iridium), designed to be used with specially designed, portable wireless phones. Iridium never comes close to the 850,000 subscribers Motorola thinks it needs to break even, and eventually declares bankruptcy in 1999, only to be saved by a consortium of companies, a new CEO, an infusion of more than $70 million from a U.S. Department of Defense contract, and renewed interest in mobile satellite communications following the September 11, 2001 terrorist attacks on New York's World Trade Center and the Pentagon. Also, in 1992, the number of cellphone subscribers exceeds 100 million in the United States. And the phrase "Surfing the Internet" is coined by Jean Armour Polly.

1993—The first all-digital Global System for Mobile Communications (GSM) cellular system is deployed in Europe. And the Federal Communications Commission announces plans to auction spectrum for new wireless communications services, including Personal Communications Services (PCS).

1994—Personal digital assistants (PDAs) and direct broadcast system (DBS) receivers are introduced. Oldsmobile introduces the first American car with a satellite-based Global Positioning System (GPS) navigation system. Also, Netscape is co-founded by Marc Andreessen and James Clark to make the Web more useful by incorporating video, audio, and animation into browsers.

1995—Online services America Online (AOL), Prodigy, and CompuServe begin commercial Internet access. SkyTel introduces the first nationwide two-way paging service. Flat-screen plasma display TVs make their debut. Also this year, Sun Microsystems introduces Java, a programming language for creating Internet-based applications; it also makes interactive features easier to use.

1996—Congress passes the Telecommunications Act of 1996. Despite unsuccessful attempts to introduce "personal communicators" by Apple Computer (the Apple Newton), Motorola (Envoy and Marco), Sony (Magic Link), AT&T (EO Personal Communicator), and BellSouth/IBM (Simon), Palm, Inc. introduces its Palm Pilot PDA, which embodies most of the features of the earlier personal communicator designs and electronic organizers.

1997—Portable DVD players hit the U.S. marketplace, initially from Panasonic.

1998—The Bluetooth Special Interest Group (SIG) is formed by Ericsson, IBM, Intel, Nokia, Motorola, and Toshiba to develop and promote short-range wireless communication systems.

1999—Cable modems are sold in stores for the first time.

2000—Third-Generation (3G) cellular communications technical standards are adopted by the International Telecommunications Union (ITU). And U.S. automakers begin offering wireless Internet access in their vehicles. The number of U.S. cellphone subscribers surpasses 100 million. Bluetooth SIG membership grows to more than 2,000 companies, and the first volume Bluetooth chipsets become available.

2001—An estimated 9.8 billion e-mail messages are being sent every day worldwide. Initial versions of Third-Generation (3G) cellphones begin to appear in Europe, Asia, and the United States. Also, two companies, XM Satellite Radio and Sirius Satellite Radio, introduce satellite-based radio networks enabling consumers (and commercial truck drivers) to listen to the same station (the services offer more than 100 stations with news and music) anywhere in the country. Bluetooth, one of the most highly touted technical innovations in recent history, begins to make its way into the market as both a dedicated product (Bluetooth-enabled headsets, for example) and an integrated feature in other, mostly portable, products (such as cellphones, notebook computers, and PDAs). JVC introduces the world's smallest camcorder; the GR-DVP3 is 1.7 by 4.5 by 3 inches.

Less Timely Timelines . . .

A cursory look at these timelines suggests that as time passes, the most significant developments—starting with the introduction of television in 1939 and followed by the invention of the transistor, the IC, the microprocessor, and the PC—were coming closer together chronologically.

As for the future, there is every reason to believe that little will change in terms of the outside influences on technological development. Lawmakers and regulators will still have their say, committees of engineers from different backgrounds and interests must still deal with technical standards for their new creations (and those of others), and industry analysts will continue to tell us what will sell, how many, and why.

What's next? Anything is possible, particularly in this post-9/11 era. Unfortunately, with the possible exception of the consumer electronics industry, true innovation seems to have slowed. Either product designers are running out of ideas, or the companies they work for simply aren't buying into them.

Adding an FM radio to a cellular phone is not a great trick—and not very exciting, especially if the manufacturer must charge an extra $60 for the earpiece to listen to the radio. However, there are some things that, down the road and technology and marketing managers willing, might just interest more consumers and give the personal technology market a much-needed boost. That is, features that consumers might actually want and use. Some of the author's blue sky examples:

2003—An unknown Chinese audio equipment manufacturer introduces a cellphone/PDA with a complete built-in weather station (thermometer, barometer, etc.); sells a million units the first week it's on the market.

2004—Cellular phone manufacturers begin to introduce models with long-hyped virtual displays, enabling users to view entire pages of text or graphics (including drawings, blueprints, and photographs) through a near-eye viewfinder integrated into the phone. The New York State legislature, which outlawed the use of cellphones while driving in 2001, introduces legislation that would make it illegal to use DVDs, MP3 players, satellite radios, electronic games, portable computers, and in-vehicle navigation systems while a vehicle is in motion. Automakers react by making campaign donations to the legislators through their in-house electronic payment systems.

2005—So many PDAs and notebook and laptop computers are now being used by companies that are concerned about the security of the data stored on these devices that several manufacturers introduce models that can only be activated by the owner's retina scan and personal voice recognition.

2006—Ericsson, which has been working with a hospital and wireless carrier in Denmark on a joint project to develop a solution for remote monitoring, follows up on an October 2001 announcement that monitoring patients with heart problems from their own homes could become a reality in Denmark in the next few years with the introduction of a cellphone/PDA model with a built-in defibrillator.

2007—Automakers begin installing wireless local networking devices as standard equipment in their vehicles after several cities announce plans to equip their street lights with remote sensors, enabling the vehicle closest to an intersection to get the green light.

2010—Several Japanese consumer electronics companies introduce a portable communications system that translates languages in real-time over global wireless networks.

2017—After more than 30 years of research, Sony announces that it is closing its Esper (extrasensory perception) laboratory where it studied the possible existence of extraordinary bio-perception, such as telepathy and clairvoyance. The head of the Sony lab said, "Of course, we are very disappointed. It seems that while mental telepathy is a very cheap form of wireless communications, it is not very reliable."

Bibliography

Scott Adams, 2001, *God's Debris* (self-published).

Michael Crichton, 1999, *Timeline*, BarnesandNoble.com (e-book).

Global Competitiveness of U.S. Advanced-Technology Industries: Cellular Communications, 1993, United States International Trade Commission.

James Hogan, 1998, *Mind Matters: Exploring the World of Artificial Intelligence*, Del Rey Books.

Marvin Minsky, 1988, *The Society of Mind*, Simon and Schuster.

Andrew M. Odlyzko, 1999, "The Visible Problems of the Invisible Computers: A Skeptical Look at Information Appliances," *First Monday* (online at www.firstmonday.org/issues/issue4_9/odlyzko).

John Rhea, 1988, *SDI—What Could Happen (8 Possible Star Wars Scenarios)*, Stackpole Books.

The Unpredictable Certainty—Information Infrastructure Through 2000, 1996, National Academy of Sciences' National Research Council.

Michael J. Wolf, 1999, *The Entertainment Economy—How Mega-Media Forces Are Transforming Our Lives*, Times Books.

Index

About the Author

Ron Schneiderman has been covering technology for more than 30 years. He is a contributing editor for *Portable Design* and *IEEE Spectrum* magazines. He was the chief editor of *Wireless Systems Design* (Penton Media), the executive editor of *Microwaves & RF* (also Penton Media), New York Bureau Chief of *Electronics* (McGraw-Hill), and the communications/consumer electronics editor of *Electronic News* (Fairchild Publications). As a freelance writer, his work has appeared in the *New York Times*, *TV Guide*, *Rolling Stone*, and *Encyclopedia America Annual*. He is also the author of six previous books, including *The Mobile Technology Question and Answer Book—A Survival Guide for Business Managers*. Schneiderman attended the University of Oregon.

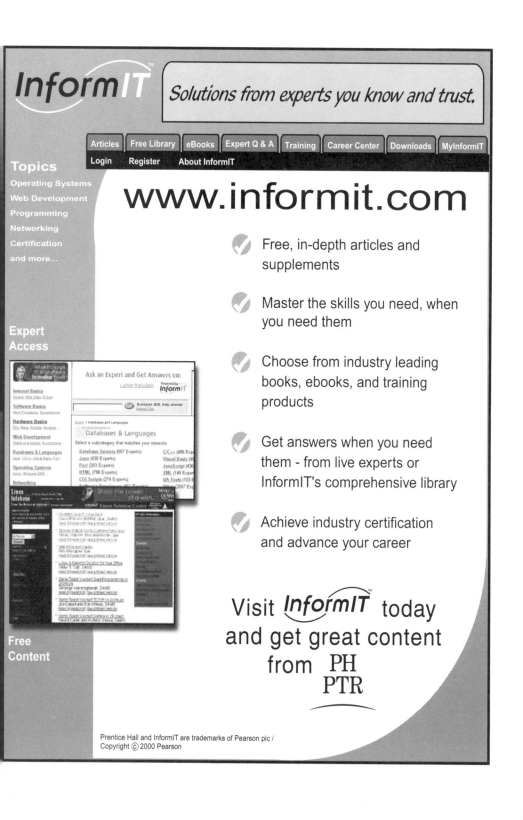

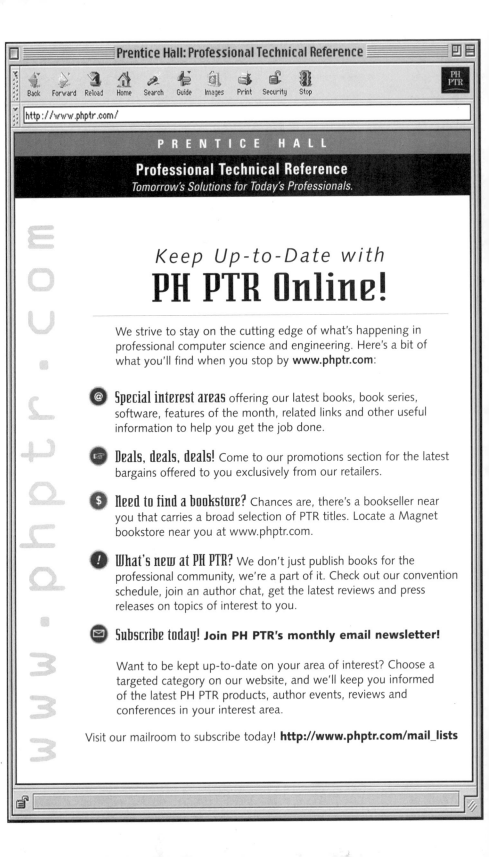